# Cabell McLean
## 1952 – 2004

I0500250

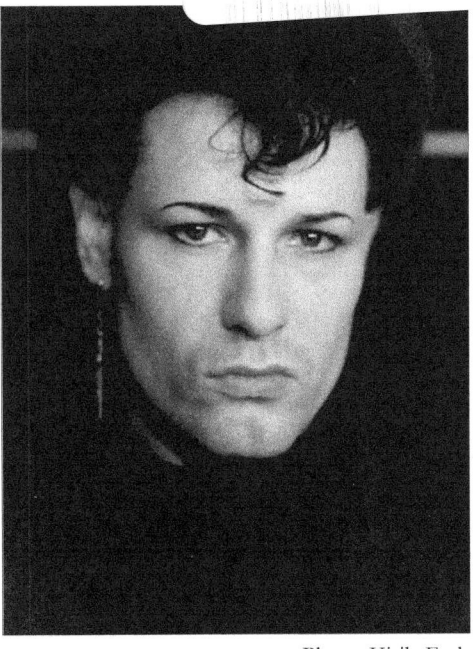

On December 1, 2004, Cabell McLean, writer and Ashé contributor, passed away due to complications from Hepatitis C. HIV-disease was listed as a contributing cause on the death certificate. He was 52.

McLean was a descendant of the visonary American writer James Branch Cabell (Jurgen) for whom he was named. While he was an undergraduate at the University of Virgina, Cabell's widow provided

Photo: Kirila Faeh

McLean with one of three keys to the James Branch Cabell room. That enabled the young writer to have access to many first editions of modern classics and origianl manuscripts. It also provided him invaluable insight into the need for a writer to understand what had come before him.

After graduation, he attended the Naropa Institute. The poet Larry Fagin recognized McLean's talent. Fagin encouraged him to show his work to William S. Burroughs. That summer McLean attended Burroughs class on screenwriting. Although he was enraptured by what he described as "the overwhelming impression of ancient wisdom," that emanated from Burroughs, he was reluctant to approach him. One night at 10 p.m. stoked by a sufficient quantity of vodka, McLean brought his oeuvre of youthful writings to the sage's apartment and knocked on his door. In a 1999 interview, he described what happened next:

"[Burroughs] opened it almost at once, looked at me with a sour expression and said, "Oh, it's you!" I could tell he remembered me from class. I was unsure what to do next, but then he stood aside and said, "Well, come on in." He offered me a drink (just what I needed!) and I took it. He was drinking vodka, and poured a tumbler nearly full, topped it off with tonic, and pushed it across the kitchen table to me where I sat. I told him I'd come to show him my work. He accepted this and opened my portfolio. My heart sank as he flipped through my carefully typed stories about the criminals and drug addicts I had known, each page receiving but a cursory glance before being flipped over and forgotten. He went through the entire collection of some twenty stories in less than two minutes!

"Is that it?" he asked. I just sat there, stunned, saying nothing.

"Very nice," he said, and I could tell he thought no such thing. I supposed they seemed terribly amateurish, and I was completely humiliated. I was already thinking about the best way to get out of there politely when he said, "Let's go out on the porch."

He stepped out onto the small, railed porch through the glass door and looked over into the Varsity Apartments courtyard. In spite of the hour, most of the apartments were active and the courtyard was brightly lit. Across the way, we watched a young boy, perhaps fifteen, naked but for a swimsuit, climbing up and around the trellises that covered the inner walls of the courtyard. "That's Beade, Spence's kid," Bill murmured to me as we watched the youthful body pull and stretch up the wall. "Like a little monkey he is. Climbs all over the walls out here all the time. I never know when he's going to climb right up and stick his head through the window to say hi." I had to admit the boy was beautiful, and said so. Bill smiled at me in a way I came to know well later, the smile of a vaudeville showman, the smile of a gombeen man, and said, "Young boys do need it special!" He laughed and put a large, heavy hand on my shoulder, and suddenly I knew everything was going to be alright."

McLean spent the next five years with Burroughs as both a student and personal assistant "to learn the craft of writing from a master craftsman." During that time, McLean paid his own expenses, drawing from a stipend from his family. He was emphatic about not accepting money from Burroughs.

McLean participated in many literary experiments with Burroughs. He recalled: "I researched these periods and places [that were incorporated into Burroughs' novels], and much of my early work with Bill involved learning his special techniques of researching a story idea. These included the usual background reading, but also included visiting locations, focused dreaming, cut up experiments, and "walk-throughs." A walk-through was when Bill and I would act out a scene to see how things might go. I always had a lot of fun doing walk-throughs with Bill. This was during the early days of his work on *Place of Dead Roads*, which he called by its working title *Gay Gun*. We'd drive out to visit sites of interest to him, places where events happened in the history of the west. There we would do short re-enactments of certain scenes, such as a gun fight, for example."

In fact the initial publication of the short story "Gay Gun" in the December 1978 issue of *The Washington Review of Books* gave both Burroughs and McLean by-lines.

McLean left Burroughs in 1983 to pursue his own career, although the two remained life-long friends and were in contact until Burrroughs' own death. McLean was always very reluctant to trade in on his association with Burroughs to gain attention. In fact he only gave one interview about his relationship with Burroughs, in spite of repeated offers to give paid interviews.

In New York, McLean became active on the alternative music scene. He acted as unofficial manager of the popular band the Stimulators ("Loud Fast Rules.") His one-time partner, Patrick Mack, fronted the Stims. Mack's early death from tuberculosis (most likely due to HIV disease) plunged McLean into a period of depression and marked the first intrusion of AIDS into his life.

When he began to see his way out of mourning, he sold the option on a screen treatment "L'Ornias." The story centered on a gender-bending demon who is described in "The Testament of Solomon" as having a taste for effeminate young men. McLean's story eerily reflected the devastation of the Gay community unleashed by the AIDS pandemic. The producers were unable to arrange financing before the option expired. In the last years of his life, McLean modified "L'Ornias" as a graphic novel script. He also collaborated with the late writer Miguel Pinero on a Miami Vice script that was not finished due to Pinero's sudden death.

However, fiction remained his dominant form of expression. Much of his work explored the New York Draft Riots. He wrote over twenty-five short stories centered on that event and the Irish gangs in New York. Those stories form the core of his yet unpublished novel, Riot. He described his interest in the Draft Riots and the Irish Criminal Gangs that had developed in New York in the preceding years. "It is....period of great change in criminal life, the advent of the first truly organized criminal groups, and the consolidation and establishment of corruption as a major part of American political life. It is also the period during which the first major organized effort at racial genocide was attempted.

That is, in fact, what the Draft Riots were: a blatant attempt by the Protestant power structure in New York City to remove the poor Catholic Irish from the city."

McLean was keenly aware of the effects of political oppression of minorities, although it was not until 1990 that he devoted his own life to political activism. Then McLean's life was turned upside down when he was diagnosed with full-blown AIDS while visiting a friend's family in Baltimore, Maryland. At the time, he prognosis was especially bleak. His T-Cell count hovered around 100 and he had PCP. He was given a prognosis that he had six months to live. However, McLean informed himself as best he could about his disease. (As a former pre-med student with a sharp intellect, he was able to make sense of his medical condition the way few patients at that time could.)

He adopted the moniker, "Lee Hardy" for this phase of his life. (His birth name was Cabell Hardy.) He developed ACTUP Baltimore's Treatment and Data Committee. The experience caused Hardy to realize that there was a lack of access to readily comprehensible information about HIV and its related disease treatments. This motivated him to form his own non-profit organization AIDS Research Information Center (ARIC), Inc. The organization handled up to hundreds of requests weekly from patients and their care-providers for explanations of existing and experimental treatments and treatment options for HIV and its related sequalae of diseases. Hardy handled each request personally. The inquiries inspired him to create *ARIC's AIDS Medical Glossary*. The publication was an exhaustive omnibus defining aspects of HIV, HIV medicine and opportunistic infections. It featured nearly 2,000 definitions. In the five years prior to the advent of widespread Internet access, it filled a critical void in the lives of many living with HIV disease. He also wrote a column on HIV treatments for the local Gay paper, The Baltimore Alternative. He was a founding member of three community advisory boards at John's Hopkins. He established the first community advisory board in the nation specifically dedicated to the treatment of children with HIV disease at Hopkins. He was a constant presence at national level treatment conferences.

McLean actually viewed his activist work as a practical application of what he learned from Burroughs. He frequently commented that all he was doing was being a Johnson. Burroughs explained the idea in his introduction to Place of Dead Roads. "A Johnson honors his obligations. His word is good and he is a good man to do business with. A Johnson minds his own business. He is not a snoopy, self-righteous, trouble-making person. A Johnson will give help when help is needed. He will not stand by while someone is drowning or trapped in a burning car." McLean took these words as gospel, and everyone around him seemed to be trapped in a burning car.

His commitment to social activism cost his literary career dearly. Excessive client demands, conference commitments, and his own failing health robbed him of valuable time that he could have spent writing. Fortunately, McLean's literary work was rediscovered by musical innovator (and "Wrecker of Civilization") Genesis P-Orridge in 1999. Orridge presented McLean's unpublished manuscripts to the committee selecting the talent who would appear at the prestigious Spoken Word Poetry Festival in Stockholm, Sweden. Even though an outstanding international reputation was prerequisite for the authors chosen to read, Hardy was selected to appear on the obvious merit of his talent. He occupied a featured spot on an evening bill and received an outstanding audience response. The reading aired on national television in Sweden. Offers to appear at similar functions throughout Europe soon followed, as did publishing offers. Unfortunately, McLean's failing health necessitated him to turn down the performance offers.

The engagement inspired McLean to write extensively about his experience with Burroughs in an autobiographical account entitled *The Machine*. A section of *Machine* appeared in *Ashé*. He also wrote many science fiction stories and even began work on a children's picture book inspired by his life-long affection for dogs.

McLean's writing was not a knock off of Burroughs. He seriously devoted himself to writing as craft, and read as many as five books a week until the last year of his life. He had a clear understanding of his personal style. He described it in the following terms. "Over the years, I think I can honestly say that I have succeeded in creating my own unique writing style, my own special take on Bill's teaching. My style now depends almost wholly upon a concise narrative, and my use of cut up is severely limited. In my work, cut ups are used to indicate extraordinary experiences: dreams, sex scenes, fights, complex action scenes like battles, and so forth. For me, the cut up is the most accurate way to describe the nature of thought, both conscious and unconscious, at times of stress, excitement, and contemplation."

In the end, the majority of his work remains unpublished. The truth is he hardly ever submitted it fro publication. He was never very good at engaging in platitudes, a quality that did not always endeared him to the literary community. Given the short span of his life, he probably didn't have the time.

McLean leaves behind his brother, Willis Hardy, Jr., of Florida, his aunt Virginia Vance, of College Park, MD, his life partner of the past 18 years, Eric K. Lerner, of Baltimore, MD, and his two beloved dogs, Butter and Biscuit.

# Table of Contents

On the Cover:

Sar Joséphin Péladan, Alexandre Seon, 1891, Oil on canvas.

Following Page:

O Grave, Where Is Thy Victory, Jan Toorop, 1892, Pencil and chalk on paper, 60 x 75 cm, Rijksmuseum.

Ashé Vol 4, Number 1, Spring 2005

# ASHE JOURNAL

www.ashejournal.com

EDITOR    Sven Davisson

ASSOCIATE    Eric K. Lerner
EDITORS    Diane Chase
Bobby Shiflett

FRIENDS OF ASHÉ

Baba Raul Canizares, Chris DeVere, Philippe Gagnon, Trebor Healey,
Mogg Morgan, Syamasundara dasa, Amara das Wilhelm

VOLUME IV, NUMBER 1
©MMV Ashé Journal

PUBLISHED BY REBEL SATORI PRESS
www.rebelsatoripress.com

ISSN: 1558-4690 (print) / 1558-4704 (digital)
ISBN: 978-1-60864-099-7

EDITORIAL OFFICES
P.O. Box 363, Hulls Cove, ME 04609

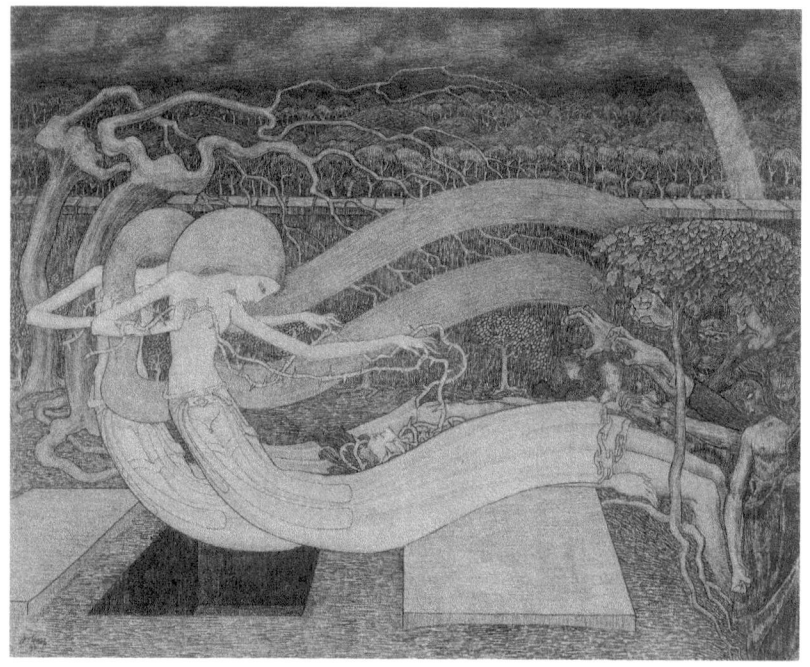

IN LOVING MEMORY OF

OF THOSE WHO HAVE GONE BEFORE

## Introduction

As the second half of the 19th century got under way, naturalism predominated French art and literature. Figures such as Emile Zola and Edouard Manet exemplify the philosophical impulse upon which naturalism was founded. Referring to Manet's work, Zola wrote, "Our art's essential aim is to objectify the subjective (the exteriorization of the idea); instead of subjectifying the objective (nature seen through a temperament)." With its roots in the century's earlier Romanticism and influenced by the sensibilities of the midcentury Pre-Raphaelites, the Symbolists arose in direct opposition to the concrete objectification underlying naturalism.

The Symbolists diverged from their contemporary Impressionists such as Monet, Cezanne and Seurat. As the two movements moved away from naturalism, the latter was influenced by the awakening of scientific discovery, while the former embraced the religiously motivated resurgence of hermeticism, myth and allegory. The Symbolists had a mutually influential relationship with the Pont-Aven School. Gauguin gave the Symbolists color and an expanded capacity for expression, while the Symolists influenced Gauguin by elevating the importance of signifiers within his work.

The official beginning of the Symbolist movement is marked by the publication of the Symbolist manifesto by Jean Moréas in the Literary

Supplement to *Le Figaro* on September 18, 1886. "Romanticism," wrote Moréas, "after having sounded every tumultuous alarm of revolt, after having had its days of glory and battle, lost its strength and its grace, abdicated its heroic audacities, made itself orderly, skeptical and full of good sense." His manifesto heralded the establishment of a new poetry that saught "to clothe the Idea in sensual form which, nevertheless, would not be its goal in itself, but which, while serving to express the Idea, would remain exposed."*

"The Idea," Moréas continued, "in its turn, must not be deprived of the sumptuous simars of external analogies; because the essential character of the Symbolic art consists of ever going until the concentration of the Idea in itself." For Moréas "concrete phenomena" did not arise of their own accord, but were, rather, "the sensual appearances intended to represent their esoteric affinities with primordial Ideas."

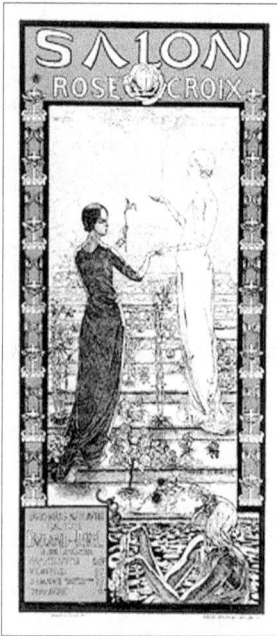

Poster, Carlos Schwabe, 1892, Lithograph, Picadelly Gallery, London

Important Symbolist poets included Charles Baudelaire, whose *Les Fleurs du Mal* is considered the first literary expression of the movement, Paul Verlaine and Stéphane Mallarmé. Symbolism was most influential in the visual arts, however, and included painters such as Gustave Moreau, Fernand Knopff, Odion Redon, Edvard Munch and Pierre Puvis de Chavannes.

It took only a few years before the movement founded on Moréas's manifesto merged with the growing interest in hermeticism, Gnostic Christianity and the occult that arose as the fin de siecle approached. Sâr Péladan and others founded a Rosicrucian-styled order whose public face was the Salon de la Rose+Croix. Their first exhibit opened in March of 1892 and included more than seventy-five exhibitors. The Salon began with an overture especially composed by Eric Satie and followed a mass at St. Germain l'Auxérrois that included excerpts from Parsifal. Carlos Schwabe designed the poster for the inagueral salon. The first Salon included the notable Symbolist artists Jean Delville, Knopff, Alexandre Séon and Alphonse Osbert.

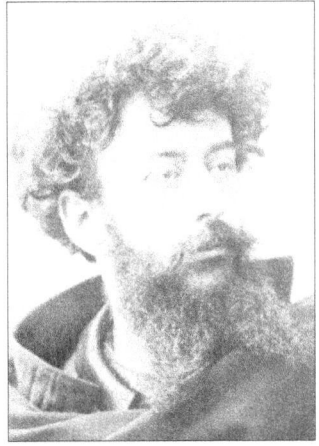

Sâr Péladan

In his accompanying book, Péladan declared his goal to be nothing less than "to restore the cult of the IDEAL in all its splendour, with TRADITION as its base and BEAUTY as its means [and] to ruin realism, reform latin taste and create a school of idealist art."†

---

*Translation by Eamon Graham, *Bohème Magazine*, 2004, II(6).

†Quoted by Robert Goldwater, *Symbolism*. (New York: Harper & Row, 1979), pp. 186-7

# The Prophets of Montmartre

*Alamantra*

T here are places of great power. On the right bank of the Seine, Montmartre gazes down over the rest of Paris. It is this place that has long been a crucible of creativity, and a refuge for the visionaries that have come to us from time to time. It is said that Montmartre was once a sacred site for the Druids. Beneath Rue La Vieuville traces of two temples built during the Roman occupation have been discovered. One temple dedicated to Mercury, the god of trade and travel and the other dedicated to Mars, the god of war and a chief deity of an occupying force.

Christened with the blood of a Saint, Montmartre literally means "Mountain of the Martyr". Saint Denis, (also known as Dionysius**)**, the Bishop of Paris was said to have been beheaded there around 272 EV. Later, another Denis, the visionary artist Maurice Denis, would emerge as 'a prophet' and noted theoretician of the symbolist school.

It has been told in "The Golden Legend" by Jacobus de Voragine that, upon being beheaded, St Denis picked up his head and carried it for several miles; all the while preaching a sermon. His journey ended at what is now called St. Denis, and a shrine was erected at the spot where he was buried. Here the Abbey of Saint Denis was founded sometime around 630 by Dagobert I, the most powerful of the Merovingian kings; and is where Dagobert and other French Royalty have been interred ever since.

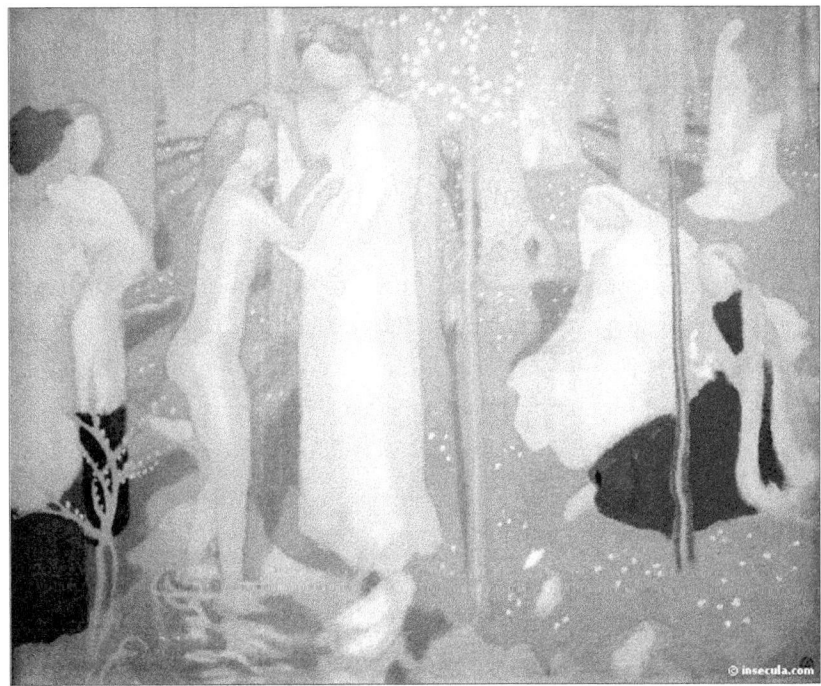

Peinture (Scène extérieure), Maurice Denis, 1897,
Metropolitan Museum of Art

That Montmartre had been the site of Denis' beheading was considered more legend than fact until 1611 when Marie de Beauvilliers, the residing abbess, discovered a crypt beneath the martyr's chapel.

Though this led to the founding of a priory there, the buildings fell prey to the French Revolution when they were auctioned off in 1794. They were demolished to make way for plaster quarries.

Louis the VI was persuaded by his wife to found a Benedictine convent at Montmartre. This was itself built on the site of an 11th century monastery. In 1147, Louis also built the church of Saint-Pierre and bequeathed large grants of land to the nuns. The rich harvest from the vineyards and fields enabled the abbey to become one of wealthiest in the kingdom. These vineyards would also fuel the birth of a bohemian renaissance.

The vineyards and windmills of Montmartre made for a pastoral setting in contrast to the worn Parisian landscapes. The poet Gerard d Nerval described it as the "finest panorama in the vicinity of Paris" in 1846 and Renoir moved into the area in 1875.

If history is to call Paris "The City of Light", then Montmartre is that light's beacon. On the Feast of the Assumption of Mary, August 15, 1534, a group of six students met with Ignatius of Loyola there to make a mutual vow of poverty and chastity, and so create the Society of Jesuits. It has been held by scholars that Ignatius' exposure to humanism at the College of Sante Barbe was fundamental to the teaching philosophy propagated by the Jesuits. Over the years, circumstance along with a unique passion long tempered by this humanistic influence would also take shape in the emerging art, literary, and theatrical expression for which Paris has achieved such renown.

The rebuilding of Paris during the Second Empire of Napoleon III caused the original inhabitants to move outward from the city center. The nunnery of Montmartre had long been known for the plentiful and inexpensive wine it produced. This combined with the fact that Montmartre was officially outside of the city of Paris and therefore exempt from its taxes made the area quite attractive to the artistic and free spirits who gravitated there.

After the Second Empire was defeated in the Franco-Prussian war, all of the revolutionist trends that had germinated in that city for a hundred years ignited in a general uprising, which culminated in the Paris Commune of 1871. That the Prussians would occupy Paris had been negotiated in the Terms of Peace at the conclusion of the war. However, the citizens of Paris remained defiant and confined the Prussian occupation to a small area of the city. Out of a concern that the citizens would arm themselves and provoke the Prussians, the Government of the Third Empire sent troops into Paris to disarm them. The National Guard refused to surrender their weapons and so the French Army fled to Versailles to declare war on Paris. On March 28th the Paris Commune was proclaimed. Proscription was ended and the army disbanded in favor of a National Guard wherein all capable citizens would bare arms in mutual support and defense. Church was separated from state and all church property was declared state property. They postponed all debts and abolished the collection of interest for debts.

The revolutionists represented a varied and diverse palette of philosophy and disposition. These anarchists, socialists and republicans were collectively known as communards and were attacked by the Army from Versailles on April 2nd, and by May 21st they had been suppressed. The French Army was ruthless in putting down the uprising and slaughtered unarmed citizens. Hundreds of communards hid in the chalk mines of Montmartre and were forever imprisoned when the Army of the Third Republic dynamited the exits.

In 1875 the foundation stone was laid for the Basilica of the Sacré Cœur (*Sacred Heart*) to commemorate the constitution of the Third Republic and as a monument for the Parisian citizens who had died during the overthrow of the Paris Commune. This was built on the butte of Montmartre and sits over Paris as a crowning tribute to Republican thought. Its architecture is based on the Roman-Byzantine style, and two bronze equestrian statues of France's national saints surmount the triple-arched portico: Joan of Arc and King Saint Louis IX.

Many in history have regarded the brief Commune of Paris as a triumph for the principles of self organization and have commended the courage of the citizens of Paris who, disappointed with their government for failing them in the war with the Prussians, asserted their right of self-governance and their spirit of defiant independence. This sense of liberty was bound to express itself as an impetus for a rapid evolution in all of the arts: Visual, Musical, Literary and Theatrical; and is one of the defining characteristics of the mood of the Fin de siecle.

In May of 1885, Victor Hugo, the celebrated writer of Les Miserables, died, and with him passed the end of an era. In his final will the great humanist, who had been revered by Republican and Socialist alike, left fifty thousand francs to the poor and refused the 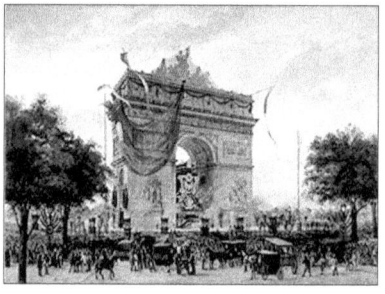 prayer of all churches. He stated, "I ask for a prayer from all living souls. I believe in God."

Children clad in Grecian costumes kept a vigil over his remains, which lay in state beneath the Arc de Triomphe. Over two million people turned out into the streets as the procession carried him to his final entombment in the Panthéon. The church had been especially unconsecrated for the event and was, instead, re-dedicated to the memory of famous men.

Victor Hugo's death paralleled the end to the Romantic period, which his work had defined. This gave way as the Symbolists led an Avant Garde toward Art Nouveau, Impressionism and simultaneously Post Impressionism. The occidental art traditions began to be influenced by the oriental, and the tradition of the artist at the easel gave way to an earnest attention to other mediums such as textiles, glass and lithography. Montmartre would become a breeding ground for the amalgamation of political, mystical and artistic influences. As the 19th century began to wind down, this quaint hillside district would become the focal point of decadent art and entertainment and the most famous artists and personalities would mingle at popular attractions like Quat'z'Arts and Le Chat Noir.

Le Chat Noir first opened its doors in November of 1881, when the artist Rodolphe Salis convinced poet Emile Goudeau to relocate the Hydropathes from the Latin Quarter café.

The Hydropathes were an eclectic society of writers, artists, and performers who had been meeting twice a week regularly since 1878. They had succeeded in publishing their own bimonthly journal, *L'Hydropathe* for a year and a half, and had been able to introduce standards that formalized the relationship between the artists and the use of the café as a venue for their works. Within two months of opening its doors, La Chat Noir was publishing its own journal.

This was illustrated principally by Adolphe Willette, Caran d'Ache and Théophile-Alexandre Steinlen, who combined macabre and infantile themes in a format of "a story without words." This Rabelaisian approach was matched by the décor of the club itself. In addition, the journal created another medium for shameless self-promotion: *"The Chat Noir is the most extraordinary cabaret in the world. You rub shoulders with the most famous men of Paris, meeting there with foreigners from every corner of the world."* The club prospered and within three and a half years they were able to move from their humble two room beginnings to a much larger and more elaborate space.

The bawdy, Rabelaisian air of the establishment was inspirational when artists George Auriol and Henry Somm constructed a small puppet theater at the Chat Noir in the fall of 1885. Somm had written a one act play called, *Berline de l'émigré* which was set in a 'family run public lavatory.' The focus of the play was on toilet habits and its sequence of buffoonery, puns and in-jokes calls to mind some of the stylistic characterizations of 'Gargantua and Pantagruel'. Within a few months this novel approach gave way to the shadow theatre that was to become La Chat Noir's greatest legacy and a favorite public attraction until the club closed its doors in 1897.

Another favorite Montmartre hangout of the emerging bohemian culture was Quat'z'Arts. Established by François Trombert in 1893, this 'cabaret artistique' is considered to have represented the cutting edge of the Avant Garde. Quat'z'Arts created an interdisciplinary atmosphere that brought together artists, composers, musicians, performers, poets, and illustrators; and where the artists enjoyed a unique and more direct relationship with the public.

The audience themselves became active participants in the event which itself became an artistic expression. Quat'z'Arts continued into the 20th century and in November of 1901 began to run the first of 64 performances of Ubu Roi. This had originally been staged at the Théâtre de l'Oeuvre in 1896, with live performers and contributions to the set by both Paul Sérusier and Henri de Toulouse-Lautrec. Still its author, Alfred Jarry, preferred to see it performed with marionettes and persuaded Trombert to host the marionette performance at Quat'z'Arts. The production, featuring the debauched antics of 'King Ubu' was a success and events like this, as well as such novel attractions like the club's collage wall-journal "Le Mur," attracted the likes of Pablo Picasso.

During much of the first decade of the 20th century, many of the artists lived and worked in a Montmartre commune called "Le Bateau-Lavoir" (meaning: "The Laundry Boat"). Picasso lived and worked there from 1904 to 1909—where he is said to have invented 'cubism.' The tenement was a gathering spot for such figures as Guillaume Apollinaire, Henri Matisse, Jean Cocteau, and Gertrude Stein; and a celebration banquet for Henri Rousseau was organized there at Picasso's studio in 1908.

Other famous names took inspiration from Montmartre and the unique spirit manifest there during the fin-de-siecle: Van Gogh, Renoir, Degas, Matisse, Redon ...the list is as extensive as it is 'impressive'. However, there is a more sublime and esoteric aspect that emerged among the artists during this emphasis of the Avant Garde. One group in particular emerged from this environment that was strongly influenced by the "synthesist" approach advocated by Paul Gauguin. They are known to history as...

## Le Nabis:

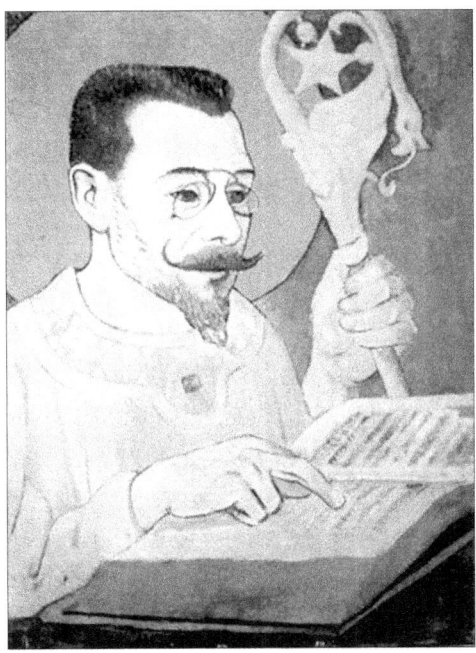

Portrait of Paul Ranson in Nabi Costume, Paul Serusier, 1890.

"It is well to remember that a picture before being a battle horse, a nude woman, or some anecdote—is essentially a plain surface covered with colors assembled in a certain order." Maurice Denis (French, 1870-1943)

(Note: The metaphysical implication of the above addresses the interpretation of meaning in the universals schemata as well. Before an object is defined as any particular thing it is a cluster of random elements arranged in a unique order. All else is an imposition of a learned or artificial categorization.)

In October of 1888 artist Paul Serusier returned to the Academy Julian. With him he brought a painting done on the lid of a cigar box that he created at Point Aven under the guidance of Paul Gauguin. It was to become known among those it brought together as "the talisman." It was a landscape, but one that departed from the naturalist or imitative style.

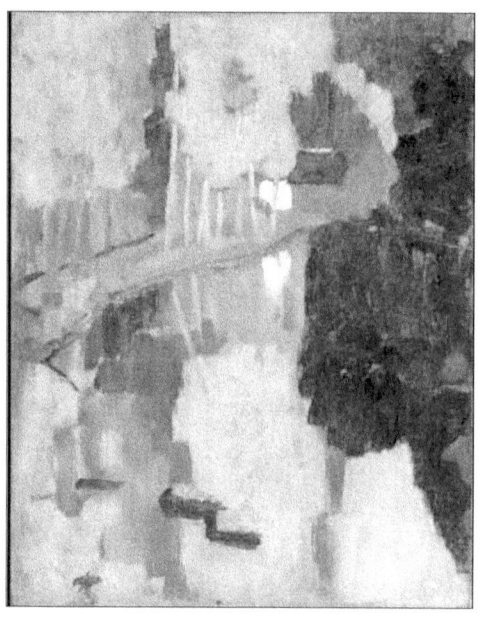

The Talisman, Paul Serusier, 1888.

Gauguin had encouraged the young painter to exaggerate his impressions, …to use pure, flat colors and to use his own symbolic, decorative logic. This was an instruction in Gauguin and Emile Bernard's new artistic style they called Synthetism. Synthetism stressed an emotional interpretation of a subject over a mere imitative depiction or re-creation. It emphasized color, line and form as an independent aesthetic value. It also taught a conscious effort to rely more upon memory and characterize bright, flat two-dimensional shapes as well as apply symbolism to explore abstract concepts. In other words, no longer would a piece of art be a simple depiction of a subject, but the subject would itself become an expression of the artist's own visionary experience. How this begins to introduce a new sort of mystical element through the projection of the artist's will or vision should be readily apparent.

Serusier enthusiastically showed the painting to his friends at the Academy Julian and shared the new ideas and technique he had learned in Brittany. This caused an excitement among the more progressive minds at the Academy and inspired vigorous debate. Four of his friends came together with Serusier to explore the new techniques, and they informally named themselves Le Nabis ('The Prophets', or more properly: 'The Inspired'.) Initially, Le Nabis was composed of Serusier, Pierre Bonnard, Maurice Denis, Henri Ibels and Paul Ranson although they would eventually number a dozen or so and be associated with other artists such as Cézanne and Redon.

Although Serusier has been credited with naming the group, it was actually given its moniker by his friend, Henri Cazalis, who is remembered as a writer, poet, mystic, critic and also a close friend of Mallarme (who was also to be a major influence on the Nabis). Cazalis had a deep interest in topics like the Kabbalah, oriental philosophy and eastern religions and had himself been dubbed: *Hindou du Parnasse contemporain.*

( \Par\*nas''sian\, *One of a school of French poets of the Second Empire (1852-70) who emphasized metrical form and made the little use of emotion as poetic material; -- so called from the name (Parnasse contemporain) of the volume in which their first poems were collected in 1866. Thus this title indicated that he was the eastern influence in that group. Add as footnote, when laying out)*

That there was a mystical influence to this group is certain, but the degree of influence such topics as mysticism, the occult, spiritualism and so on had over the group as a whole has been an issue of speculation. Of the dozen or so artists that one finds within the group there is a variety of spiritual and political beliefs ranging from Theosophy to orthodox

Christianity, Buddhism and anarchism. There were two basic inclinations in the group. There was the mystical esoteric side of art as represented by Ranson and Serusier who were theosophists and then there were the others like Vuillard and Bonnard who remained aloof from the group's theoretical discussions and quasi-mystical pretense. They found work in creating sets for the emerging cabaret scene at Chat Noir and illustrating periodicals such as Revue Blanche.

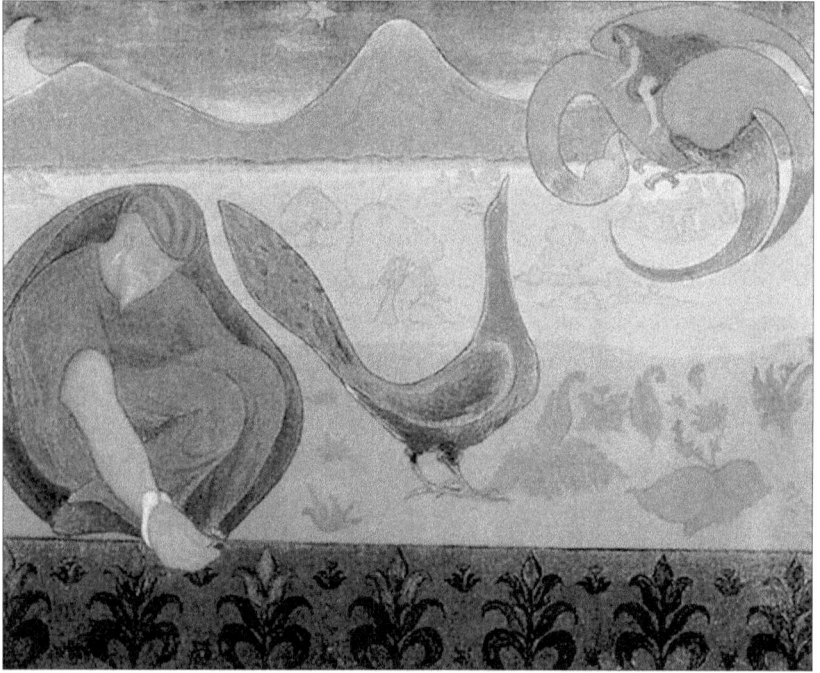

Nabi Landscape, Paul Ranson, 1890, Oil, Josefowitz Collection.

What united Les Nabis was their belief that the most important function of art is to provide a sense of unity or continuity. Their credo was "the simplification of form and the exaltation of color." To this end they worked in a variety of mediums believing that even functional day-to-day accessories should be stylized and imbued with the artistic vision.

They viewed themselves as initiates of a brotherhood devoted to exploring and portraying the pure sources of art, primitive feeling and sincere emotion. They used devices such as heavily decorative borders to enclose and partition the subject of their works and define them as expressions of the artist's vision rather than a mere recreation. The goal was to 'seek beauty outside of nature' and so they were interested in not corrupting the sense of wonder or mystery contained in any given thing including 'the ordinary,' which they felt could be and should be transformed. They made it their purpose to integrate art into all walks of life and created wallpapers, fabrics, tapestries, stained glass, pieces of furniture, folding screens and stage sets, reuniting artistic vision with daily craft. Their abilities reflected a wide range of visual interpretation as well, employing Japanese color woodblock prints with modern printmaking techniques.

The group was loosely organized around dinners that occurred at fairly regular monthly intervals between 1888 and 1896. These dinners originally started at "l'Os à Moëlle", a café in the Brady Passage and were later also held at Paul Ranson's Montmartre apartment. At these events, the attendants would dress in 'oriental costume' or long white tunics and each artist would bring an 'icone,' a piece that he had recently done and they would discuss their work, theatre, literature and other topics of social interest. They would often read aloud authors such as Mallarme, Maeterlinck and Baudelaire.

At the beginning of the dinner, the presiding Nabi would raise a staff that resembled a bishop's crozier and intone:

"Sounds, colors, and words have a miraculously expressive power beyond all representation and even beyond the literal meaning of the words."

In addition to the monthly dinners Paul Ranson and his wife, Marie-France, who was known as 'the light of the temple,' began to host Saturday afternoon gatherings for the group where Gauguin was known to make an appearance from time to time. Their apartment on Boulevard du Montparnasse was known as "Le Temple" and was also referred to by the Nabis, along with George Lacomb's Versailles studio, as one their two 'ergasteriums'. (a Greek word meaning: a place where work is done.)

They would sign their correspondence to each other with the phrase:

D.T.P.M.V.E.M.P. Dan ta paume mon verbe et me pensee. *In your palm my word and thought.*

It was through such arcane and archaic phrases and gestures that they created and ritualized their endeavors. Ranson would bestow upon each new member a "picturesque soubriquet" or name by which he would be known within the group. Serusier was known as 'Le Nabi 'a la barbe', Bonnard was 'Le Nabi-Japonard,' and Denis known as 'Le Nabi aux belle Icones,' Lacombe as 'Le Nabi Sculpteur' and so on, each member having a name that reflected how he was seen within the group.

The fruit of their association created a general styling that submerged the artist's particular personality though not his vision. This was initially successful although in an 1894 letter to Jan Verkade, Serusier wrote that Vuillard, Roussel, Bonnard were relying on themselves and that personality was destroying the style created by the Nabis.

In fact, Vuillard, Ker-Xavier Roussel, and Bonnard later renounced the Nabis doctrines in favor of their own unique styles whereas Ranson, Serusier and Lacombe continued to hold to the Nabis aesthetic which carried its influence toward the opening of Academie Ranson in 1908. When Ranson died in 1909, the other Nabis, especially Marie-France (Ranson's wife), Denis and Serusier kept it open and it is where Serusier began to expand on his interest in employing the golden ratio in his artwork.

The Prophets remain an excellent example of the variety and evolution of creative thought, which has become a primary tradition of the Montmartre district; a school embracing all schools whether they be mystical, mythological or purely aesthetic. This is the story of a place and of a time where genius rubbed shoulders with genius and created a legacy of inspiration for those who embrace the human condition and its endeavors. They are the fruit of a moment where time meets itself, where the death of one age gives birth to a new one. I would like to close this article by serving you a brief quote from Hillel Schwartz's "Century's End: A Cultural History of the Fin De Siecle From the 990s through the 1990s:

> The new phrase insisted Berlin journalist and philologist Fritz Mauthner in his 1890/91 essay on on fin de siecle as adjective and presumptive noun, had begun as a rather empty reference to some vague anticipations of the century's end, but the very act of giving a name to those anticipations had made possible a way of thinking about one's time that had been unavailable before. Originally an allusion to indeterminate feelings, fin de siecle had become an active agent for historical thought. Mauthner was developing philosophy of language, of which Ludwig Wittgenstein would soon be the peerless exponent, that knowledge and perception are tightly interlaced with language, and that their horizons expand only and conjointly with new acts of naming. Himself beset with inescapable feelings of culmination and threshold, Mauthner was impressed that fin de siecle had arrived a decade in advance of the next century. He was eager to 'outfit for the twentieth century' by rethinking the common

past, which meant reconsidering the language in which that past had been cast. (Hillel, 165-166)

Le Nabis were truly the prophets of this rethinking of the application of symbol and aesthetic and, driven by the impetus of being alive in an age that has been called "the best of times and the worst of times," they were able to bring forth light from the midst of an otherwise perceived encroaching darkness that lingered through the dawn of a new century and gave birth to both world war and global connectivity. Their legacy was passed on through the other artists and creators, who knew them personally or through their work and who used this perch on a quaint Parisian hillside to cast their light into the world.

References:

Buisson, Sylvie and Christian Parisot. *Paris Montmartre*. Paris: Terrail, 1996.

Schwartz, Hillel. *Century's End: A Cultural History of the Fin De Siecle From the 990s Through The 1990s*. New York: Doubleday Publishing, 1990.

Silverman, Debora L. *Art Nouveau in Fin-De-Siecle France: Politics, Psychology and Style*. Berkeley: University of California Press, 1989.

Whitfield, Sarah and John Elderfield. *Bonnard*. New York: Harry N. Abrams, Inc. 1998.

Nabis, http://www.kilidavid.com/Art/Pages/Movements/nabis.htm (accessed 11/04)

Nabis by Sharon Himes, http://artcafe.net/ah/bonnard/nabis.html (accessed 11/04)

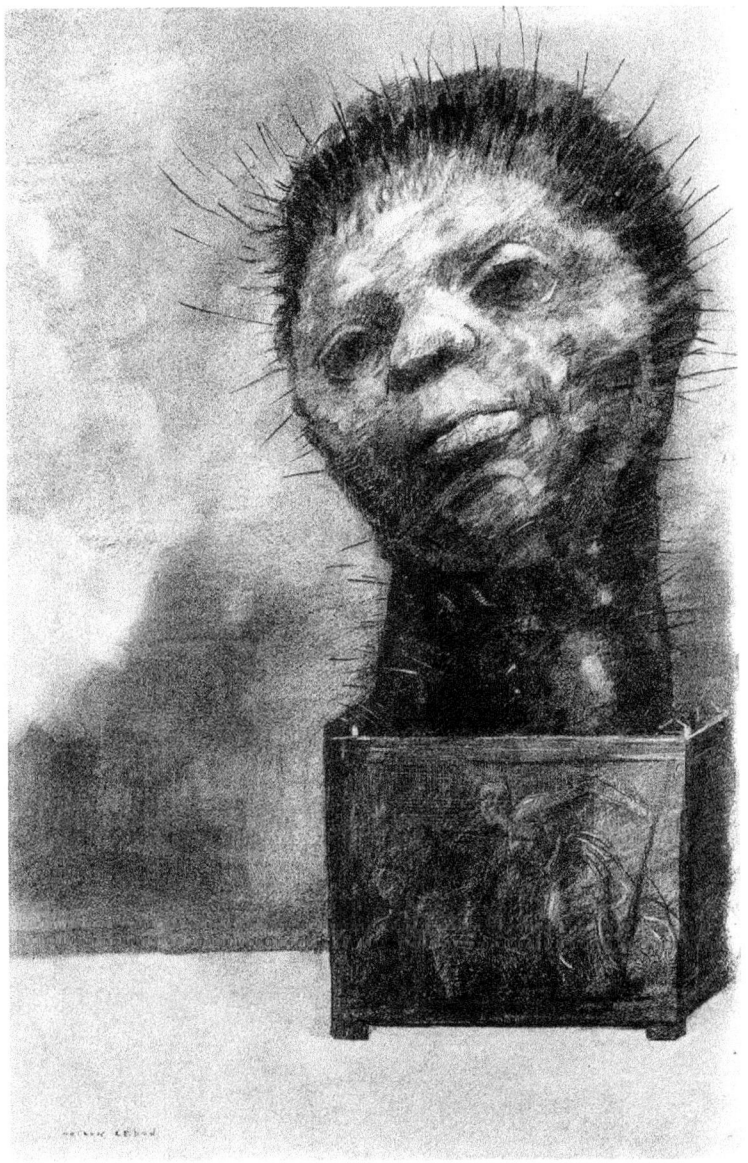

Cactus Man, Odilon Redon, 1881, Charcoal, 49 x 32.5 cm,
The Woodner Family Collection, New York

# The Plastic Ideal:
## The Androgyne In *fin de Siecle* Occulture

*Sven Davisson*

A preoccupation with fundamental duality is rooted deeply in the philosophical history of Western civilization. This notion of dual existence, or binary opposition, most commonly manifests as a tension between male and female, masculine and feminine, but extends to a greater force-relation of humans and the external world. In one-way or another, metaphysicians have long sought a means of reconciling or escaping this dualism. Often, historically, the solution has been resulted in a configuration of the androgyne as a spiritual ideal—an ideal being that exists outside of the split domain of the male and the female. Below, I will examine three modern mytho-religious traditions that centered on this search for a solution to this proto-duality.

Most of the Western mystical tradition rests on myths that humanity developed out of a primal void. The Bible begins, "In the beginning of creation, when God made Heaven and earth, the earth was without form and void." (Genesis I:1-2) Medieval alchemists portrayed this void as the *prima material* given form by Mercurius, who was often depicted as a hermaphrodite. (Singer, 131) Qabalistic cosmology rests on the concept of Ain Soph, the veils of chaos (nothingness) that exist before the first emanation of the Divine (Kether on the tree of life). Within these three creation myths, division is a necessary precondition of creation. Organizing the chaos of the void depends upon the development of a binary system. Nothing coalesces into the point, creating tension between the form and the formless, which, in turn, splits the point into two forming a dynamism. The search for an escape from this dualistic state has formed one of the great pursuits of philosophers, mystics and occultists alike. This current manifested strongly in the fin de siecle occulture, with the Symbolist artists of the Salon de las Rose+Croix, and in the 20th century with the notorious occultist Aleister Crowley and the futuristic philosopher William S. Burroughs.

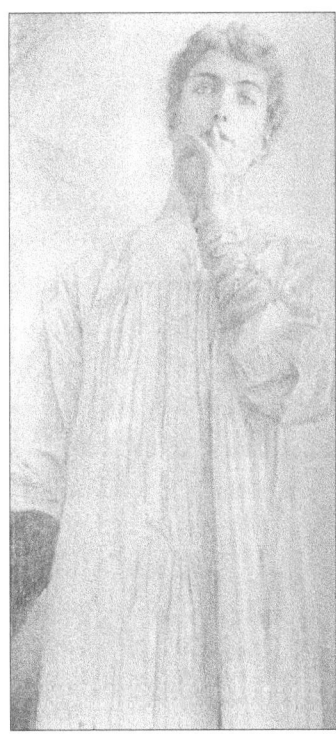

Silence, 1890
Pastel; 85 x 41.5 cm
Musees Royaux des Beaux-
Arts de Belgique, Brussels,
Belgium

In his analysis of early man, Arthur Evans sees the sexes as living very separate lives. Stone age people lived apart from each other in sexually segregated houses and, at times, even villages. (Evans, 15) According to Evans research, the sexes only came together for procreative purposes, while recreational sex was primarily same-sex. Although several religious artifacts from this period depict hermaphrodites, within the practical levels of religious ceremony, there generally appeared to be room for only one mystery and that female. There is evidence from numerous cultures that the first male shamans were transgendered, being initiated as female. In some cases, male shamans even underwent ritual castration in order to receive the mysteries of the cult.(Evans, 17)

Medieval Qabalists were among the early proponents of androgyny as a solution to the problem of an existence based on duality. The Qabalists describe three levels of 'negative existence' preceding the first emanation of the Divine. Crowley poetically described these three states as "The Ante-Primal Triad That Is Not-God: Nothing is. Nothing Becomes. Nothing is not."(Crowley, 10) Out of this chaos God created pre-Edenic man, Adam Kadman, the archetypal androgyne. Rabbi Simeon writes in *The Zohar* that "the man of emanation [Adam Kadman] was both male and female from the side both father and mother for he was all light."(Singer, 87) The human became complete, with the second creation of man in the Garden and his split into male and female. *The Zohar* explains that a person in this nonwhole form is not capable of receiving diving blessing:

> Therefore we know: what is only masculine or only feminine is called only part of the body. But no blessing rules over a faulty or incomplete thing, but only over a complete place, not one that is divided, for divided things cannot long endure or be blessed. (Singer, 161)

The Kabalists' solution to this "faulty" state is the androgyne, a careful combining of the male and female natures within each person. This action thus creates a unified being worthy of the blessings given over a complete place." The apocryphal gospel according to Thomas, utilized by many contemporary Gnostics, exemplifies this requisite for benediction:

> When you make the two one, and when you make the inside like the outside and the outside like the inside, and the above like the below, and when you make the male and the female one and the same, so that the male not be male nor the female female; and when you fashion eyes in place of an eye, and a hand in place of a hand, and a foot in place of a foot, and a likeness in place of a likeness; then will you enter [the Kingdom]. (Lambdin, 129)

In the latter half of the nineteenth century, the artists of the Symbolist movement exalted the androgyne image as the human ideal. The Symbolist artists attempted to break from the cult of realism, which they felt incapable of finding meaning, due to intentional limitation. Des Hermies, in J.K. Huysmans' *La Bas*, outlines the faults the Symbolists found in Emile Zola and his associates:

> The fault I find with realism is not the dull monotone of its ponderous style, it is the uncleanliness of its compositions; the fault I find is its having embodied materialism in Literature, and having glorified the democracy of Art! . . . What a low-minded theory, what a petty, narrow system! Voluntarily to limit oneself to the off-scourings of the flesh, to reject the suprasensible, to deny the visionary not even to realize how the mysticism of Art

> begins at the point where the senses cease to
> help us! (Huysmans, 1)

The movement away from realism toward a new religious art manifested
clearly within the artists of the Salon de la Rose+Croix. For the Salon's
founder, Sar Joséphin Péladan, and artists such as Jean Delville, Georges
Minne, Armand Point, Fernand Khnopff, and Jean Dampt the
androgyne played a fundamental role in their idealized mythic
configuration. The androgyme, as differentiated from the hermaphrodite
employed by others of the period, represents no less than the absolute
goal of human spiritual evolution. By depicting the androgyne, the artists
of the Salon de la Rose+Croix were creating/recreating a form of
mystical art that served, at least in the mind of Peledan, to reestablish the
role of religious art in intellectual society. Sar Péladan proclaimed
categorically, "the androgyne, is the plastic ideal!" (Pincus-Witten, 44)

In 1884 with the collaboration of several prominent occultists
including Stanislas de Guaita and Papus (Gerard Encausse), Péladan
formed the Rosicrucian order le Ordre de la Rose+Croix+Kabalistique.
The intent of this organization was to strip the system of Kabalistic
magic of the frivolous accumulations of centuries and revitalize the
Western mystical tradition. Péladan soon became uncomfortable with
the Eastern influences within the ideology of the order, and in his Salon
of 1890, announced his departure from the order. On 23 August 1891,
article 9256 in *Les Petite Affiches* made the schism legal, with the formation
of the Association de l'Ordre de la Rose+Croix du Temple et du Graal—
otherwise known as the Rose+Croix+Catholique. With the financial
backing of Count Antoine de la Rochfoucauld, Paladan wished to move
away from the former order's Orientalism and return to the Papist
church. (Pincus-Witten, 77) On a more practical level, the break with
Guaita allowed Péladan to embody explicitly his religious ideals in the

order structure and gather together a collection of artists with similar views toward the primacy of the androgyne archetype.

Throughout his involvement with the Rose+Croix+Kabalistique and the Rose+Croix+Catholique, Sar Péladan experimented with the theme of androgyny in his literary works. The androgyne plays an important role as the ideal within his 1884 novel *Le Vice Supreme* as shown in Leonora's dialogue with Antar. She advises the artist to "make an angel, without sex, the synthesis of a young man and a young woman." (Olander, 118) In 1888 Péladan's *Istar* was published, with a frontispiece by Khnopff, depicting a woman, head thrown back in ecstasy and completely devoid of surrounding except for an extremely phallic flower that grows toward her groin. Péladan described Khnopff's frontispiece as "the emotional nude, that is to say, the expression of the model apart from its surrounding." (Pincus-Witten, 68) The hint of muscles and wide jaw that Khnopff gave the model evoke a haunting, androgynous tone. They strengthen her without reinforcing her feminity. While the frontispiece of *Istar* is an example of the way in which Khnopff's women differ from the traditional androgyne, the angle of the head and the inclusion of the florabunda suggest a subtle cross between the androgyne and the femme fatale, containing glimpses of other thematic depictions prevalent in the Symbolist movement. Jean Delville, also an exhibitor at the Salon de la Rose+Croix, noted in his comment on Khnopff's work:

> Khnopff has created a type of ideal woman. Are they really women? Are they not rather imaginary feminites? They partake at the same time of the Idol, of the Chimera, of the Sphinx and of the Saint. They are rather plastic androgynes, subtle symbols, conceived

according to an abstract idea and rendered
visible. (Howe, 48)

This passage shows that Delville saw in Khnopff's work a combination
of several precursors of the androgynous form: the Greek
hermaphrodite, the Babylonian Tiamat, and da Vinci's saints.

Eighteen-ninety saw the publication of Péladan's *L'Androgyne*, the
plot of which centered around the androgyne Samas. Alexandre Seon
drew the frontispiece for this work. It depicts, in the words of Péladan:
Above the strange rocks of the Brehat, lickjed at by the waves, there rolls
in the sky in piece of the moon, the head of the androgyne Samas,
stupefied by the sexual enigma. (Pincus-Witten, 71)

Since *L'Androgyne* is an autobiographical depiction of Péladan's
childhood in a Jesuit school, Péladan is equating himself with the
androgyne. By presenting Samas' head in the place of a celestial body,
Seon's drawing exalts Samas, and through him Péladan to the role of
divine being. This representation also strengthens Péladan's view of
himself as magus, since the moon symbolizes, in its relationship to the
tides, the power over the flow of nature.

Following the legal establishment of the Rose+Croix+Catholique,
Péladan began preparations for the first exhibition of the Salon de la
Rose+Croix scheduled for the following year. Fernand Khnopff was
among those exhibiting in the first Salon and continued to exhibit in the
Salons of 1893 and 1894. His work embodies two of the major themes
within the Rose+Croix movement, the androgyne and the mage.
Péladan felt that Khnopff's philosophy was closely aligned to his own,
which led him to proclaim in *Salon de Champ de Mars* of 1893 that
Khnopff was an "Admirable and Immortal Master." (Pincus-Witten, 153)
In the Salon of 1893, Khnopff exhibited "L'Offrande" and "I Lock My
Door Upon Myself," both of which contain references to the
androgynous nature of their subjects. Khnopff created this androgynous

feeling by giving his women a massive jaw, "a jaw so massive," in the words of art historian Micheal Gibson, "that Mussolini himself, with his ham-sized howl might have envied them." (Gibson, 109) The over emphasizing of the model's jaw gives her an atypical female face.

In "I Lock My Door Upon Myself" Khnopff used the model's clothing to create her sexual ambiguities through de-sexing her body. Her long hair and a subtle softness of the features are the only elements that outwardly denote her sex. The female in L'Offrande possesses even fewer clues that allude to her gender" since unlike the model in I Lock My Door Upon Myself, the model has her hair back, forcing her face to stand alone and appear all the more ambiguous.

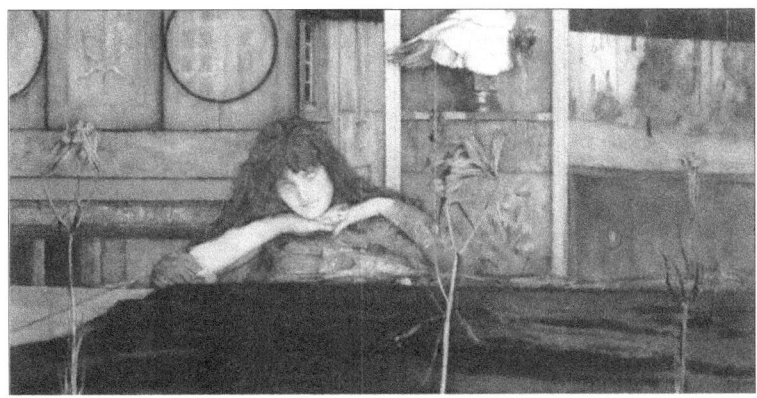

I Lock My Door Upon Myself, 1891, Oil on canvas; 72 x 140 cm, Neue Pinakothek, Munich, Germany

The inclusion of the arum lily in "I Lock My Door Upon Myself" serves to reinforce the androgynous interpretation of the painting. Khnopff employed this particular lily throughout his work to allude to androgyny, it reappears in "Arum Lily," "The Secret Reflection," and "Le Reflet Bleu." The arum lily belongs to the class Gynandric, which is distinguished by having both male and female characteristics, and is thus the floral embodiment of Khnopff and Péladan's ideal. These women also embody the chaste ideal of Péladan's androgyne. It is impossible for these women to satisfy sexually, since both are 'removed from sexual physicality into a moment of isolation and introspection. This looking inwards displays the role of the magus, since magic is a search for internal union, especially when coupled with the depiction of the androgyne. The model in "I Lock My Door upon Myself" rests her arms on a table which has a coffin like appearance. This particular use of death imagery is more than a reference to suicidal contemplation; it represents the power that the magus has gained over the mysteries of life and death. The lilies in the paintings foreground can be viewed as a further reification of the magus's harmonious understanding of life's progression. They move from birth to death reflecting the magician's acceptance of natural laws.

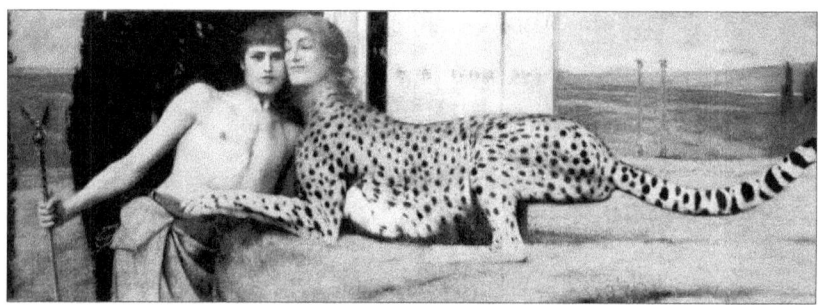

Des Caresses, 1896, Oil on canvas; 50 x 150 cm, Musees Royaux des Beaux-Arts de Belgique, Brussels, Belgium

Through the iconography of his work, Khnopff linked the androgyne and the magus with the internal search of the artist. He drew the comparison between himself and the magus most strongly in his depiction of Oedipus in "Des Caresses" (1896). Like Gustave Moreau in "Oedipus and the Sphinx," Khnopff depicted the victorious Oedipus as an androgyne. In both paintings, Oedpus carries a staff symbolizing his newly gained dominance over the physical world. In Khnopff's depiction, he wears a wreath of flowers in his hair drawing on the image of the laurel wreath, serving to establish further that the Oedipus of "Des

Caresses" is indeed Oedipus the victor. He has answered the Sphinx's riddle and gained the wisdom of the magus. This knowledge has taken him outside the world of opposites and recreated him as the androgyne. For the Symbolists, Oedipus is both prototype and allegory. He exists simultaneously as the mage and the archetypal androgyne. For Khnopff he represented more than the androgyne and the mage. He equated these two with the artist. Péladan echoed Khnopff's visual idealism in his religious/artistic rhetoric, when he exclaimed, "Artist thou art priest."(Howe, 53)

Khnopff's painting and Péladan's writing attempted to explore other levels of reality perceived by the initiate. As Charles Morice points out, "Art is not only revelator of the infinite, it is also the very means to penetrate into it."(Howe, 53) Since Khnopff considered all nature but reflections of higher realities, it was through this search, both internal and external, that he derived the androgyne as ideal. Art became the means of attaining the desired state of androgyny.

For Péladan art's most important role was that of transcendence. In *L'Art Idealiste et Mystique* he wrote, "I believe I have seen in the aesthetic emotion a luminous and heightened equivalent of the emotions of passion; and at a certain attitude of impression, art averts sin."(Howe, 49) In Péladan's conception sexual desire formed the greatest enemy to spiritual growth. Article VII of the Rose+Croix+Catholique's constitution reads "The order has one single motivating goal: to ruin sexual love, passion and to substitute the abstract and aesthetic rites,"(Howe, 141) This "motivating goal" stemmed from the androgyne's perceived,[1] dependence on initial realization of sex or sexual potential would destroy the androgyne by bringing it down to the material realm of physical desire. Péladan explained, "the androgyne exists only in the virgin state; at first affirmation of sex, it resolves to the male end the female."(Olander, 120) This split caused by sexual awakening draws greatly on Péladan's background. In *The Symposium*

Plato points to the sin of the Hermaphrodites as the trigger to their split "for our sins, God has scattered us abroad." (Hamilton & Cairsis) Within the Kabalistic structure, the fall of Adam Kadman is precipitated by his corruption into physicality.

## References:

Crowley, Aleister. *The Book of Lies*. York Beach, ME: Samuel Weiser, 1984.

Evans,.Arthur. *Witchcraft and the Gay Counterculture*. Boston: Fag Rag Books, 1978.

Gibson, Michael. *The Symbolists*. New York: Harry N. Abrams, 1984.

Hamilton, Edith and Huntington Cairsis. *The Collected Dialogues of Plato*. New York: Viking, 1961.

Howe, Jeffrey W. *The Symbolist Art of Fernand Khnopff*. Ann Arbor: UMI Research Press, 1982.

Huysmans, J.K. *La Bas*. Paris: Collection "Le Ballet des Muses", n.d.

Lambdin, Thomas O. "The Gospel of Thomas," in *The Nag Hammadi Library*, James M. Robinson, general editor. San Francisco: Harper & Rowe, 1978, pp. 124-138.

Pincus-Witten, Robert. *Occult Symbolism in France: Joséphin Péladan and the Salon de la Rose+Croix*. New York: Garland, 1976.

Singer, June. *Androgyny*. New York: Viking, 1976.

# An Early OTO Lamen From France?
# The Influence Sar Péladan

*Presented by Jonathan Sellers*

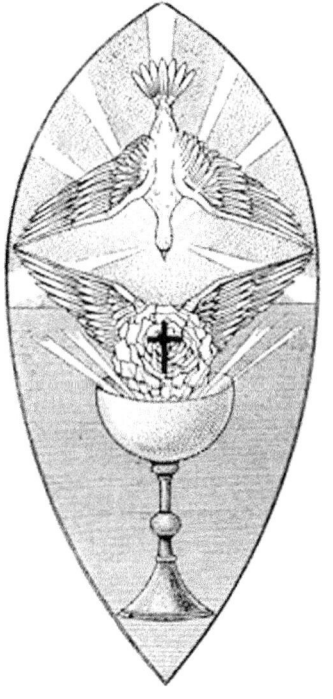

These images were discovered in the book entitled *L'Art Idéaliste & Mystique: Doctrine de L'Ordre et du Salon Annuel des Rose + Croix*, by Sar Péladan, published by Chamuel in 1894c.e., one year before Kellner is said to have established the O.T.O. in his home turf. The full title page has been reproduced on the next page and detail enlarged to the right. In it we see the Banner of the Templars, the Beauseant; the Rose + Cross, and the Sangraal. This comes from the original R+C Order that Péladan was associated with: The Order of the Rose Croix, the Temple and the Grail.

The Mitre above the Lamen is reminiscent of the Babylonian Mitre Hats, which in turn are modeled after the DuKu Mounds in the Temples, and the Original Teachers, the Apkallu, of which Oannes was the original. This fits Péladan's usage of Babylonian symbolism in his writings.

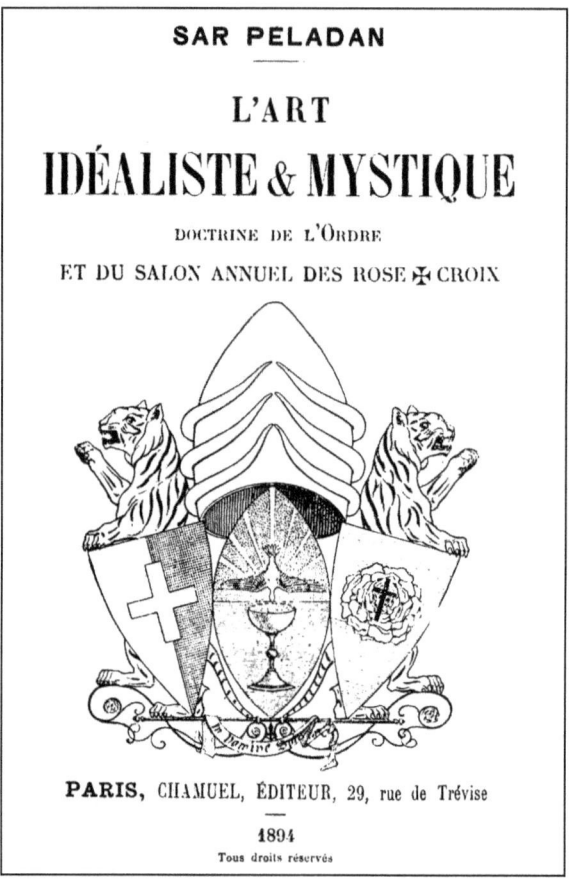

Original material reprinted with kind permission from
the Antiquities of the Illuminati
http://www.antiqillum.com/

## Elle est seule

*The Sar Joséphin Péladan*, excerpt from *La Vice Suprême*

Plein d'ombre alanguie et de silence berceur, clos à la lumière, clos au bruit, le boudoir circulaire a le recueillement rêveur, la somnolence douce, d'une chapelle italienne, aux heures de sieste; buen retiro, semblable à l'étage d'une tour ronde, sans baie à ses murs elliptiques, ou cloutée d'argent aux plis, la pourpre héraldique étale, en un satin violet plein de rouge, son deuil royal et sa magnificence triste.

Aux portières de velours, s'étouffent les voix du dehors et le plafond s'évide en un dôme, d'où le jour tombe, arrêté et affaibli par un vélarium bleu. Dans cette crypte mondaine dont la demi obscurité rend, par places, le violet presque noir, de grands lys s'élancent autour d'une dormeuse, -où, écrasant délicatement les coussins, la princesse, couchée sur le dos et sans pensée, songe, avec l'abandon de corps et d'esprit, des heures esseulées.

Sur ses formes parmesanes, le peignoir de soie violette a des froissements pareils à des moues de lèvres, à des caresses timides et effleureuses.

Un bras que la retombée de la manche dénude, encouronne sa tête aux cheveux roux et lourds, l'autre pend avec des flexibilités de lianes, des souplesses de lierre et le dos des doigts pointus touche la peluche rase du tapis.

Par un bayement de l'étoffe la gorge apparaît, filigranée de l'azur des veines qui transparaissent.

Les seins très séparés et placés haut sont aigus, les mules tombées, les pieds nus ont cet écartement de l'orteil que la bandelette du cothurne fait aux statues: et le sortir du bain amollit de matité douillette tout cet éphébisme à la primatice. On dirait l'anadyomène de ces primitifs qui, d'un pinceau encore mystique, s'essayent au paganisme renaissant, un Botticelli où la sainte déshabillée en nymphe, garde de la gaucherie dans la perversité d'une plastique de stupre; une vierge folle de Dürer, née sous le ciel italien, et élégantisée par un mélange de cette maigreur florentine où il n'y a pas d'os, et de cette chair lombarde où il n'y a pas de graisse.

La paupière mi-close sur une vision entrevue, le regard perdu dans les horizons du rêve, la narine caressée par des senteurs subtiles, la bouche entr'ouverte comme pour un baiser, -elle songe.

D'une robe couleur du temps, ou d'un coeur qui la comprenne, d'infini ou de chiffons? Dans quelle contrée du pays bleu, à la porte de quel paradis perdu, son désir bat-il de l'aile? Sur la croupe de quelle chimère, prend-elle son envolée dans le rêve?

Elle ne songe à rien, ni à personne, ni à elle-même.

Cette absence de toute pensée énamoure ses yeux, et entr'ouvre ses lèvres minces d'un sourire heureux.

Elle est toute à la volupté de cette heure d'instinctivité pure, où la pensée, ce balancier inquiet et toujours en mouvement de la vie, s'arrête;

où la perception du temps qui s'écoule, cesse, tandis que le corps seul vivant s'épanouit dans un indicible bien-être des membres. Ses nerfs au repos, elle ne perçoit que la sensation de sa chair fraîche, souple, dispose; elle jouit de la félicité des bêtes, de ces vaches de Potter, accroupies dans l'herbe haute, repues et qui reflètent une paix paradisiaque dans leurs gros yeux clignés.

La princesse savoure délicieusement l'extase de la brute; elle est heureuse comme un animal. Ses yeux en l'air regardent sans voir, le blason des d'Este, brodé sur le vélarium, et l'aigle d'argent couronnée, becquée et membrée d'or la regarde aussi, et semble crisper et roidir son allure héraldique, au-dessus du lazzaronisme de boudoir qu'elle plafonne.

Les lys, les fleurs royales, les fleurs pures, élancent, sereins et augustes, leurs tiges droites des pieds de bronze, et leurs calices d'argent, pistillés d'or gouachent la tenture de pourpre, de tons chastes et nobles.

De ses mains glissé, un volume s'étale, les feuillets en éventail.

Les accalmies absolues de l'intelligence et de la mer, sont brèves dans les hautes têtes et sur les grandes plages: le flux de la pensée reconquiert vite le corps un moment quitté. Lointaines, les images et les vagues montent, agitées et successives, et reprennent à leur repos d'un moment, le sable déjà sec et brillant des grèves, et le cerveau déjà vide et sans souffrance.

La buée qui s'élevait de la baignoire gazant sa nudité, flotte encore dans sa tête, où se fait un lever paresseux et lent des idées.

Dans ce réveil de l'immortel de l'être, où les brumes d'une aube s'évaporent, domine seule distincte, une phrase lue, qui revient, se répète obsédante, ainsi que ces hémistiches de vers oubliés qui poursuivent le lettré et ces airs entendus dans le lointain d'une vesprée que l'oreille, comme une boîte à musique, a gravés; semblable, aussi, au répons sonore de litanies balbutiées dans une somnolence de dévote, ou bien au refrain d'une ballade dont on ne sait pas les strophes: "Albine s'abandonna, Serge la posséda, le parc applaudissait formidablement." à ce chapitre où toutes les sèves en délire éclatent en un cri du rut, la princesse n'avait pas vibré. Cette bestiale ardeur n'éveillait rien dans ses sens délicats et raffinés de décadente.

Elle avait tourné d'une main froide ces pages enfiévrées, mais la curiosité, chez elle analytique, avait été intéressée par ce tableau d'une sensation inconnue, d'un sentiment plus inconnu encore.

La femme qui lit un roman, essaye, par un instinct fatal sur son âme, les passions du livre; comme elle essayerait infailliblement, sur ses épaules, la mante de forme rare qu'elle trouverait sur un meuble, aimant à se retrouver dans l'héroïne. Exceptionnelle, la princesse eût souffert de se voir écrite; et à lire Balzac, elle s'irritait pour les coins d'elle-même qu'elle y trouvait révélés.

Satisfaite, dans le soin de sa gloire, d'être indemne des ivresses animales de la sexualité; confirmée dans la rareté de son caractère, elle reçoit une louange des disparates qu'elle se découvre et sa supériorité s'augmente de tout ce qui la dissemble des autres.

Dans son passé, aucune frondaison de paradou; dans son souvenir, aucune figure de Serge, aucune.

Tout à l'heure, l'eau tombait en perles de sa nudité, et elle se complaisait aux lys de sa peau que nul baiser ne rosit jamais; maintenant une volupté qui a manqué aux pharaons et aux Césars, lui vient de la continence de ses reins, de l'impavidité de son coeur: l'impériale satisfaction d'avoir fait toute sa volonté sur soi-même.

Elle n'est, ni Sémiramis, ni Cléopâtre. Son nom illustre n'a sur elle que le prestige des ancêtres; l'histoire ne saura pas si elle a eu lieu: ce n'est qu'une grande dame de nos jours et du faubourg saint-Germain. Mais contemplant ses vertus solides comme des vices, ses vices calmes comme des vertus, elle se répète le *divi herculis filia*, de Ferrare. Car elle est elle-même le monstre qu'elle a vaincu, et invincible aux omphalus, son âme pleine de passion, son corps pétri de désirs, elle les a modelés, de son pouce long, à la spatule volontaire, d'après un idéal pervers d'Artémis moderne. Elle a vécu selon une idée: c'est sa gloire.

Le mouvement lyrique de sa superbe se calme; elle évoque lentement l'un après l'autre, les détails dont la vie est faite.

En entrant dans l'hypogée du souvenir, elle reçoit cette bouffée d'air froid et humide, qu'ont les lieux d'où la lumière et la vie se sont retirées; et la fadeur poussiéreuse et moisie des choses vieilles, lui impose son vague attendrissement.

Confusément s'éveillent: l'écho des mouvements dont le coeur a battu, une impression posthume des sensations d'autrefois, une vie retrouvée des personnages et des actes dans leur cadre, et avec, au cerveau, le retour des pensées d'habitude, aux yeux l'humidité des larmes, jadis pleurées.

Elle contemple au lointain, du haut de son orgueil, le panorama du temps défunt, et faisant présent son passé, ressuscite toute sa vie morte.

# Erik Satie

Erik Satie was born in Normandy in 1866. At age 17 he entered the Paris Conservatory, though he left after only studying a year. Later, at age 40 and already a respected composer, he would enroll Schola Cantorum, where he studied with Albert Roussel and Vincent D'Indy. Satie aligned himself with the Symbolist art movement, becoming the composer for the Salon de la Rose+Croix. Satie composed a fanfaire of trumpets for the Salon's opening exhibition in the Spring of 1892. His best known works are Trois Gymnopedies and the Gnossiennes series (reprinted in part here). In addition to his own compositions, Satie inspired contemporaries such as Claude Debussy and modern 'minimalists' such as Philip Glass and Michael Nyman. Satie died in Paris in 1925.

# GNOSSIENNE
### (1890)

*à Roland MANUEL*

*No. 1*

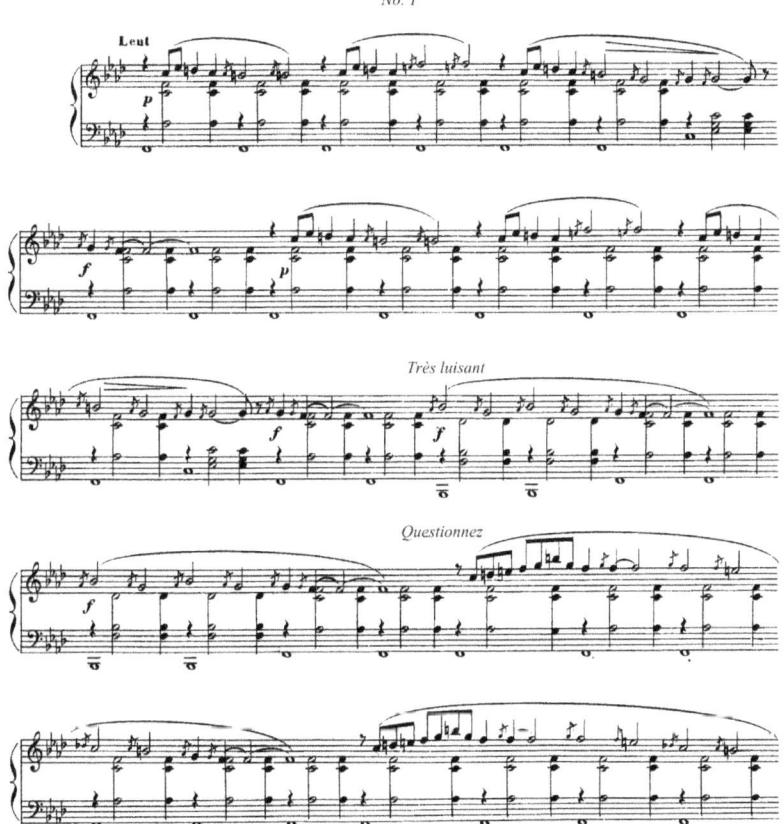

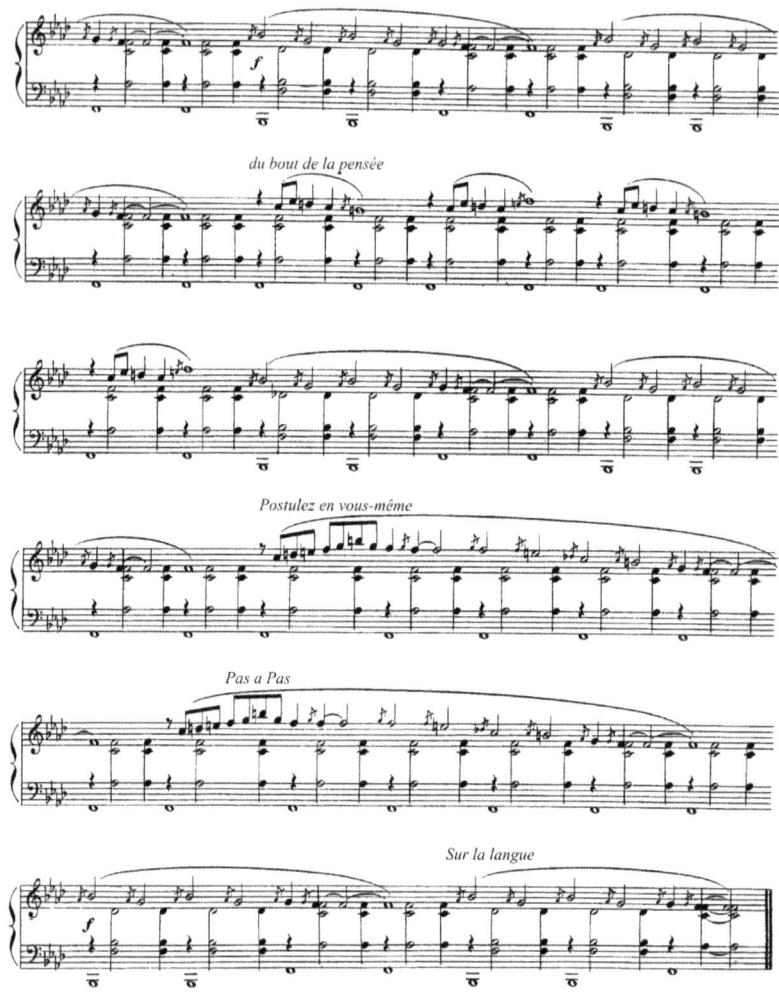

# GNOSSIENNE
### (1890)

*No. 2*

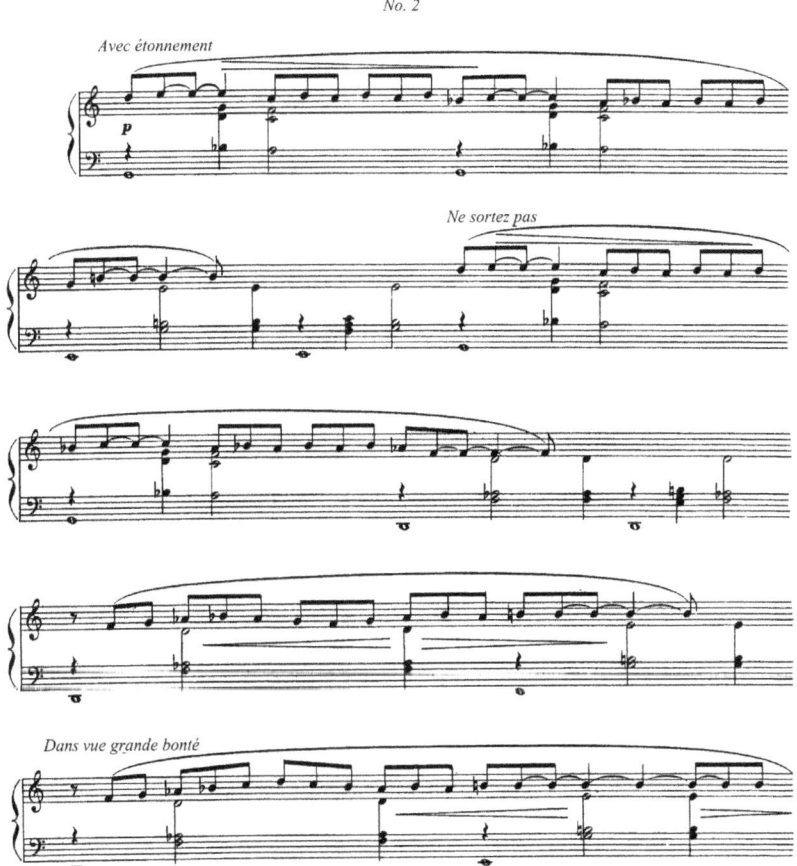

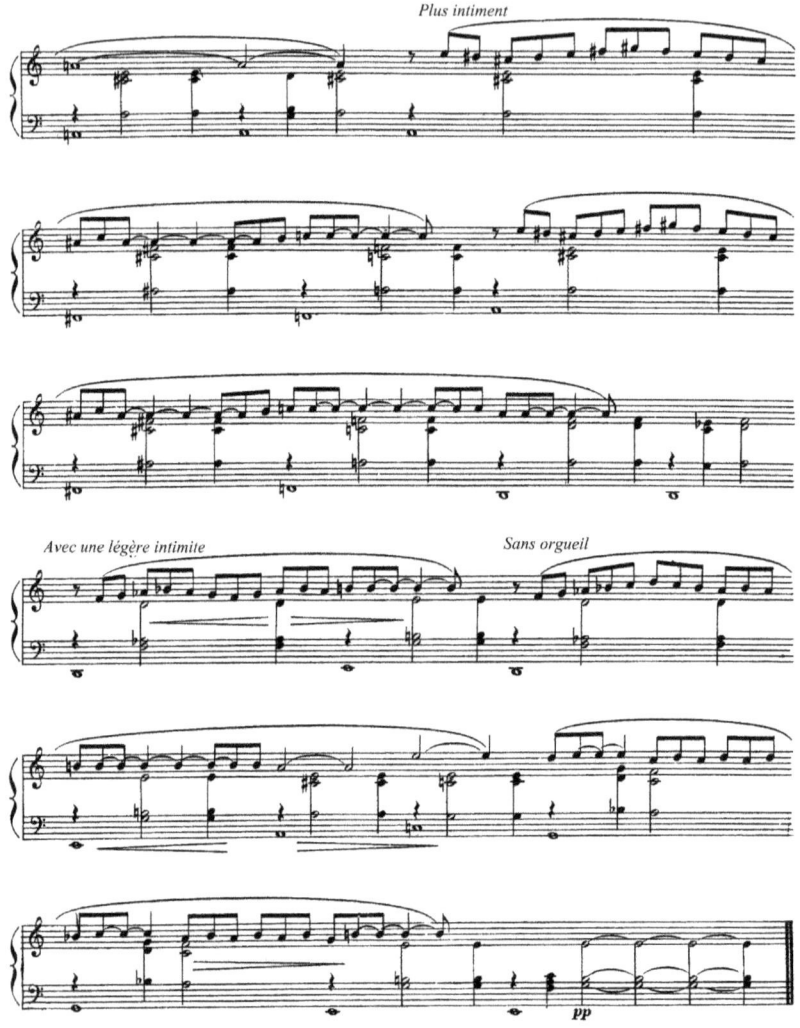

# GNOSSIENNE
### (1890)

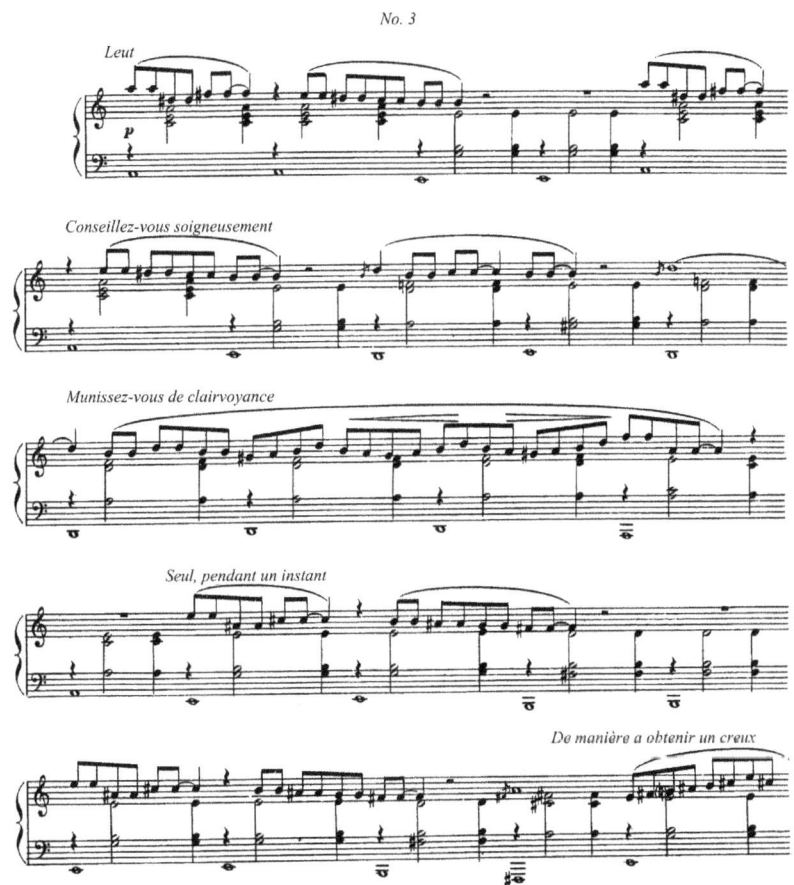

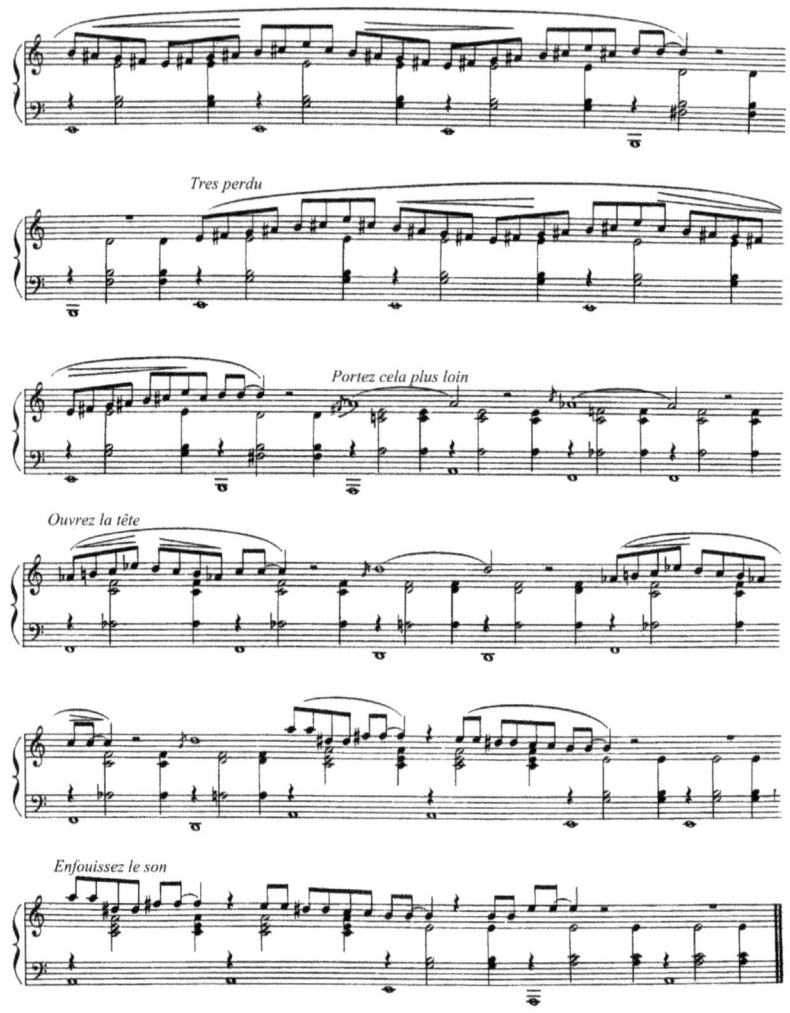

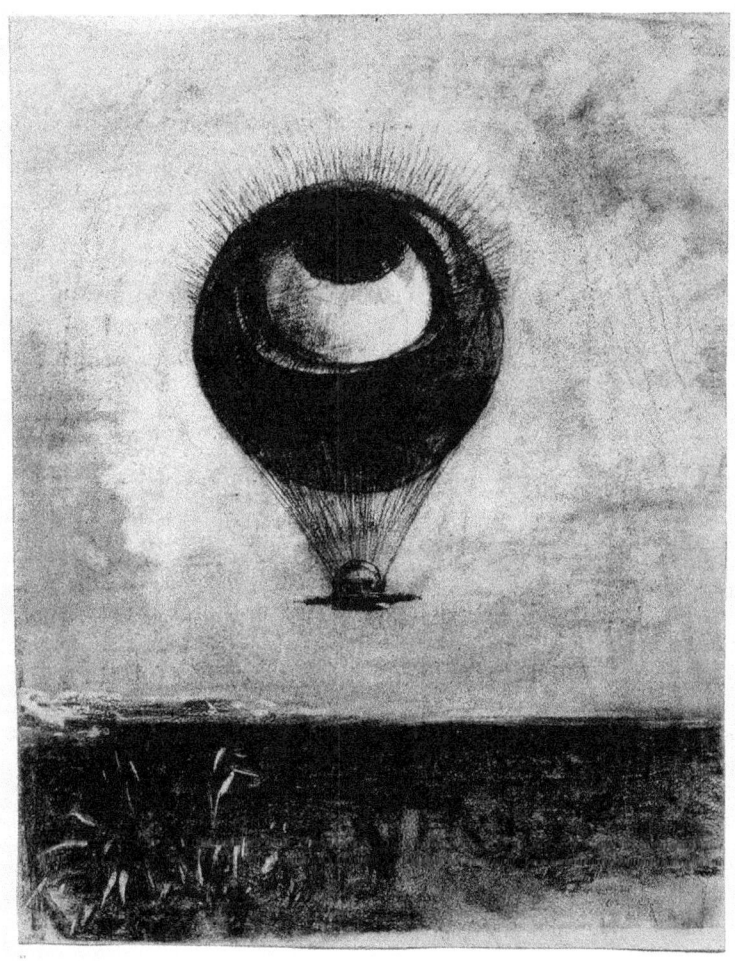

*L'oeil, comme un balloon bizarre, se dirige vers l'infini,* Odilon Redon, 1878,
Charcoal, 42.2 x 33.2 cm
The Museum of Modern Art

# Arthur Machen and the Trials of the Aesthete

*Adrian Eckersley*

W ho, or what, are artists? What is the nature of imagination's gift - and is it really a gift at all, or might it be a curse? Artists[i], after all, hold converse with things which are not: they summon voices out of the air, or conjure landscape and likeness out of nothing. A glance at some folktales reveals that an interest in the moral status of the gifted artist goes back a long way, and shows that in earlier times poetic power was connected with the underworld. Thus the German minstrel-poet Tannhauser drew his power of song from his sinful underground life in the Venusberg, and comes close to being damned for it. Similarly, the Scottish Thomas the Rhymer drew his power of poetic prophecy from his visits to underworld Elf-land and the special favour of its queen. These examples may remind us that in the traditional collective mindset, artists may be holy, or they may have some whiff of damnation about them.

In the middle years of the nineteenth century, most saw the artist as holy. Many felt the rising tide of industrial materialism as dehumanizing, and saw imagination as a comforting antidote to its factual brutality. Some understood imagination as a gift sent by God so that humans might know him more perfectly.[ii] The artist's work was essentially like the priest's; both nourished belief in what was not immediate to the senses; thus the Pre Raphaelite painters liked to depict Biblical scenes in the photographic terms most credible to their contemporaries. However, as the century wore on there was much lightening up. The later Pre Raphaelites began to paint scenes not from the life of Christ, but from classical Greece and Rome, scenes which evoked the pagan values of those societies, and could shock older mid-Victorian sensibilities. These avant-garde artists adopted the creed of 'art for art's sake', so much more liberated than the earlier 'art for religion's sake'. They called themselves aesthetes, and made a cult of beauty beyond morality. If the aesthete artist was still a holy man, he was a pagan holy man, not really holy at all to decent Christian folks. Nevertheless, the artists got away with it, mainly as the later nineteenth century was an era in which the older, harsh standards of public morality were felt to be inhumane, and were effectively in decline.

The aesthete movement began in the 1860s, and grew steadily in strength. Its climax came in the first half of the 1890s, the era of the *Yellow Book*[iii], a time of broad but fragile permissiveness. However, in 1895, rather dramatically, the permissive moral climate darkened, due to a savage and rising backlash. The event most often taken to mark this shift is the fall of Oscar Wilde. If any one figure personified the new spirit of permissiveness arising in the 1890s, it was Wilde. He was hugely successful and fashionable too. He had sharpened the subtle amoralisms of aestheticism into urbane and crackling wit, and through his 1890s plays, *Lady Windermere's Fan* (1892), *An Ideal Husband* (1895) and, above all, *The Importance of Being Earnest* (1895), he reaped a glory which focused a massive notoriety upon him, which he loved and courted. Having thus become a very public but on that account very vulnerable figure, Wilde sued the Marquis of Queensberry for the libel of imputing then-criminal homosexual activities to him. Wilde's libel suit failed, and the ensuing criminal counter-action ended in his very public disgrace and imprisonment. Yet, tragic as it was, Wilde's fall signified more than merely the punitive dishonouring of one man: his light and often provocatively flippant treatment of potentially heavy 'moral' matters made him very much the personification of the 'naughty nineties' artist, and so his dethroning may also be read as an attack upon a set of stances and attitudes common to a much wider group, an attack which would lead eventually to a cultural paradigm shift.

Wilde's fall can easily be seen as a kind of first cause of this change in moral climate. However, it may also be understood as the result of forces already in motion. The factor which concerns me here is a rising disapproval of the permissive artist by the world of science, which, as will emerge below, had the power to depict him as something far worse than a mere 'bad boy'.

The roots of this opposition lie far back in 1859, when Charles Darwin's *Origin of Species* proclaimed the theory of natural selection, which gave credibility to the doctrine of evolution. Darwin's work led to the gradual triumph of evolutionary theory, including the concomitant idea of human descent from some ape-like ancestor. But along with the idea of evolution came its flip-side: degeneration.[iv] According to the evolutionists, humanity had climbed above the animal kingdom, and might climb still further. But there was also the danger of sinking back, of evolution taking a turn backwards towards the apes, and this was what that word, degenerate, implied. Degenerates were, arguably, part of an incipient species that was different from the rest of us.

Just like the idea of evolution itself, the idea of the degenerate throwback pre-dated Darwin, though it drew a huge legitimacy from his work. Building on its foundation, social Darwinist thinkers tended to see the more successful human groups, whether defined as races or classes, as more advanced in evolutionary terms: thus for example the successful middle classes were seen as more evolved than the urban poor, and Europeans as a whole more evolved than 'savages'. Late nineteenth century criminology drew heavily on these ideas: the idea that the criminal was a kind of evolutionary throwback was explored and comprehensively documented through experimental observation by the leading Italian criminologist, Cesare Lombroso. The common criminal could be recognized, according to the school of Lombroso, by a variety of physical telltale signs which included asymmetrical features, low forehead, jutting eyebrows and so on. These were obvious, visible degenerates.

Much energy was spent, in the decades after the publication of *Origin of Species*, in restoring human species-pride by exploring and proclaiming with ever-greater precision the differences between human and animal. It became widely believed within the increasing army of Darwin's followers that the most fundamental difference between animals and humans was the human moral sense.[v] Animals didn't have a moral sense; they merely acted in their own interest – but humans could and did act altruistically, for the good of the group rather than the selfish individual. People of a religious disposition saw the moral sense as, like the imagination, a gift from God, but many of the scientists committed to evolutionary theory stressed that this moral sense, whose most obvious outward sign was the ordinary human need for the approval of others, was evolution's most recent gift to humanity, and in any evolutionary downward sliding it was the first thing that would disappear. Thus there would be some people who lacked the obvious features of the low criminal, but who nonetheless had a huge potential for criminality as they had no moral sense. These were termed 'higher degenerates' and their danger to society lay as much in the greater scope of their ability as in their capacity to disguise themselves as ordinary men or women.

There was an increasing tendency in the 1890s to see many if not all artists and writers as part of this dangerous group. In his book *The*

*Man of Genius* [vi] Lombroso argued that the moral sense, though it was the defining characteristic that separated human from beast, could have an inhibiting effect on creativity. Those without the moral sense might have what we now call psychopathic tendencies, but through their very lack of inhibition they might also be the most original thinkers of their generation. Lombroso argued this link between genius and degeneracy using examples drawn from both the scientific and artistic culture of the nineteenth century. Thus for example he listed as degenerate the poet Charles Baudelaire, whom he accused of pathological mental instability, obsessive fame-hunger, and "morbid passions"[vii] in love. There is a flavor of the witch-hunt about the book; just as supernumerary nipples were once signs of devil-following, so at that time not only physical symptoms but casts of mind and factors in behavior were adduced to demonize in medical terms.

Lombroso has arrogated the right to judge Baudelaire the man, his behavior, his emotions, his sexual preference for "ugly and horrible women"[viii] but he makes no judgment about his work. His most dedicated follower, Max Nordau, medically-trained but a keen participant in the cultural scene too, did not shirk this task. In his book *Degeneration*[ix], published in Britain in1895, the year of Wilde's fall, he treated not only the traits of character of his artist-contemporaries as medical symptoms, but also the works themselves. Nordau accused the modern artists and writers of the day - aesthetes, gutter-realists, PreRaphaelites and French impressionists alike - of being degenerate, and gave the qualities of their works as evidence for his argument. At the centre of contemporary art and literature he sees artists who are mentally hyperactive, hysterical, dream-obsessed, incapable of dealing in reason, structure or meaning. In his view, these degenerate artists were incapable of a focused, selective attention, and this led to the overexcited visions of mysticism, often tinged with a "morbidly irritated" sexuality which cannot be controlled, as the blood-supply to overexcited cells cannot be turned off.[x] He also saw this 'degenerate' art as something approaching a conspiracy. In his view there was an ongoing collusion between degenerate artists and admiring degenerate public, who were working together to ensure the triumph of a kind of culture, which would create others in its image, undermining the moral rectitude of the state.

Nordau's influential work represented a broad swathe of post Darwinian opinion, and provided authority for a witch-hunt on the degenerate artist. Thus in 1895 it was not just Wilde who was on trial, but all permissively-orientated avant-garde artists. As a consideration of fiction-texts such as R.L.Stevenson's *Doctor Jekyll and Mr Hyde* (1884) and Bram Stoker's *Dracula* (1897) may persuade us, there was a fear abroad at the time of the beast in human clothing. The artist himself could be fitted-up for the role as clearly as any of his characters.

Arthur Machen was a writer of fantastic and supernatural fiction whose career was checked by this dramatic shift in literary climate in 1895; yet from this check came his finest piece of fiction. Born in 1863 the son of a village clergyman, in Caerleon-on-Usk, a small town in the South Wales border region of Gwent, Machen was a natural scholar but his family was too poor to for him to follow his father's footsteps to Oxford.[xi] Instead, he went to London while still in his teens, officially to become a journalist but in reality to live a life dedicated to literature. In his early work the rebellious young man rejected the very language of his own time, preferring instead to write in archaic and 'fantastickal' seventeenth century prose. Then suddenly, in 1890, he dropped this approach, took on the urbane style of utterance of the aspiring young fiction writers of his time, the language of R.L.Stevenson and Arthur Conan Doyle, and began to write quite racy stories, which brought him some success.

Published by John Lane, in his notorious Keynotes series, with cover designs and illustration by the very shocking Aubrey Beardsley, Machen's work was very much part of the avant-garde scene of the first half of the 1890s. Superficially, what makes it so is the playful but normative urbanity of its style and the way narrative is handled. Like the Sherlock Holmes stories of his near-contemporary Arthur Conan Doyle, the narration is urbane and evenly paced. Tales begin almost universally in cozy London surroundings, yet their development takes the reader to the outermost reaches of the human heart, of urban social geography, or both. In the early 1890s Machen had a detective figure like Holmes: Mr Dyson, student of human nature, who is often to be found dining with his acquaintance in the best restaurants of London's West End, yet who has also intimate knowledge of the city's obscurest byways.

Yet Machen is more clearly a member of the 1890s avant-garde than Doyle, not through his urbanity, but through the places his fiction visits. Whereas in the Holmes tales we are saved from the terror of the terminally unfamiliar because there is always in the end a solution to the mystery, Machen's outcomes are less cosy. There are disturbing, exciting entities – society women of demonic parentage, substances which plunge the user into the witches' sabbath, obscure surgical procedures that can bring us face to face with a terror not so easily contained. But what makes Machen so completely a member of the avant garde of his time is the way his writing engages with sexuality.

I shall give two examples. First, his 1894 novella "The Great God Pan"[xii]: the central figure is a woman whom the reader is invited to see as descended from the devil. It is established in the text that she, Helen Vaughan, is alluring and promiscuous; yet encounters with her leave her lovers white faced, gasping, suicidal. We are never told what happens in the bedroom, but the facts of the case are functionally placed before us in such a way that we must try to imagine what happens there. Machen's fictional technique is to hide everything, yet simultaneously to make us strain to see.

A second example: in the masterly 1890 short story "A Double Return"[xiii], a married man who has been away for some time returns to his wife in London to discover that she believes him to have returned already, the night before. We may choose to read the tale as one of the supernatural, the stalking of a doppelganger, and the story encourages us to see things this way, by for example letting the hero believe he has glimpsed himself from a train. But if we are adults we will pass through this reading, and though not encouraged to do so will come to understand that an impostor disguised as the hero has spent the night with his wife. The couple are both deeply shocked by their discovery - then a curtain falls. There is brief allusion to the 'manner of conversation' which ensues between them, then a throwaway ending merely informs us that the wife had died and the husband has emigrated. The story positively encourages meditation upon what happens in bedrooms, upon how far sexual partners should or could be able to recognize one another, yet nothing of this is enunciated. Again, Machen uses the trick of combining extreme reticence with large doses of sexual suggestiveness.

The permissive dispensation under which these stories flourished was truly fragile. Their enormous reticence suggests the sense of restraint which lurked around matters pertaining to sexuality, while the obsessive nature of the curiosity they invite suggests the explosive potential of what is held in check. Machen's work in the early 1890s thus suggests in an almost structural way that sexuality is a demonic force. Considering the detail will suggest much the same. The beast in human form, that most post-Darwinian entity, is already present in the example discussed above: the trickster who spends the night with the wife in "A Double Return" is just such a creature, spreading his seed in despite of the rules, offending against altruism, and showing Lombroso's precise combination of talent, amorality and lack of concern for others. Other male figures in Machen's work are gripped by an equally furious aberrant sexuality. The demon-woman of "The Great God Pan" enters the world through the machinations of a sadistic scientist, who inflicts an operation of his own devising upon a young servant girl who is indebted to him. The text lingers disingenuously upon her innocence as she submits to his vile practices, "the feeling of submission strong upon her, crossed [...] arms upon her breast as a little child about to say her prayers"[xiv]. In a companion-piece, "The Inmost Light"[xv], the sinister Doctor Black inflicts a similar operation on his wife, to remove her soul. Machen's work of this time portrays scientists as perverts, drooling with sadistic lust to perpetrate acts of moral outrage and physical outrage upon lovely young women. Yet there is classic ambivalence afoot: the reader is invited to condemn the disgusting sadism of the scientists, but the way these scenes are described invites the reader to share the very excitement which is simultaneously condemned. As so often, the fierce and condemnatory moralism exists side by side with what it condemns. Nordau's accusations of hysteria would sit easily here.

Machen is himself at this time prepared to play dangerous games with the concept of the "artistic", illuminating its potential for acquiring immoral overtones. One of the narrators of Machen's 1895 frame-novel *The Three Impostors* presents himself to the reader as an 'artist' of crime. The tale this narrator tells, "The Novel of the Iron Maid"[xvi] concerns a collector of instruments of torture who has an unpleasantly connoisseurish, if 'artistic', relish for his collection. He is destroyed by a horrific accident with the implement of the title: familiarly, the sadism of the reader is invoked in the just punishment of that of the collector.

Fiction is a fragile platform for the ushering in of liberal or permissive attitudes. When a story is judged horrifying or disgusting, readers may easily disavow it or turn against it. A writer may try to do the same, claiming that he wrote his text only to assuage an appetite in the public, but he is less likely to be taken seriously. In 1895, Machen might have been damned merely through connection with the avant-garde and ultimately Wilde: his work had been illustrated by Beardsley, as had Wilde's *Salome*. But these connections are beside the point: Machen's work was quite capable of being judged unhealthy on its own merits, and was judged so. This fact illustrates clearly that the moral backlash of the later 1890s was not aimed only at homosexuality, but at all or any whose texts could be judged permissive.

Machen's fiction between 1890 and 1895 allows a homogenous grouping: all is urbane, exciting, rich in ambivalence, hysteriogenic. In 1895 he recognized that this modality was played out, and was looking to do something new. There is no clear proof that Machen ever read Nordau, but the text he came up with, *The Hill of Dreams*[xvii], often considered his finest work of fiction, seems to respond to Nordau's accusations. *The Hill of Dreams* is, perhaps defensively, much less hysterical than the work of the early 1890s and, furthermore, goes a long way towards adopting the perspectives of the scientific enemy. This is particularly surprising when one bears in mind Machen's hatred of scientists, vaunted in the tales discussed above.

The novel's hero is a young writer, Lucian Taylor who, unable to engage with the contemporary world, eventually fails and dies. Machen was not the only writer at around this time to engage with this theme of the artist who cannot succeed. George Gissing's 1891 novel *New Grub Street* shows us two not dissimilar figures, the young novelists Edwin Reardon and John Biffen, both of whom like Lucian end up dead: but we can be fairly sure that Gissing is pointing the blame for this waste upon the unresponsive world, not upon inadequacies of the writer himself. *The Hill of Dreams* approaches this point with a rich ambiguity.

It becomes gradually apparent that Lucian is a degenerate. Early in the novel, on a blisteringly hot summer's day, he climbs the hill of the title, falls asleep or into trance, and is assailed by a vision of the goddess, which we may also interpret as a sex-dream. The side of Lucian which responds to the erotic goddess of imagination is presented to the reader as a faun, the half-man half-goat entirely-sexualized Pan-figure from Roman times. This faun is, at any rate at first, not quite Lucian's self but is a living potential within him, as Hyde is within Jekyll. But it is important; the faun that lives hidden within him is the essence of the young man's imaginative power, to write. Though this is a far more sympathetic treatment of the artist than anything in Nordau's book, Nordau's ideas are nevertheless endorsed: Lucian is a writer because something atavistic, something of the throwback, lives vitally within him. However, he can reap no benefit from this; the alter-ego faun compromises the young man by resolutely insisting on living within its own world rather than joining Lucian in his. If we need that sort of label we may see Lucian as schizoid, but this undersells the subtlety with which the novel allows us to engage with two not-quite-conflicting but also not-quite-complementary realities, which become irreconcilable only very late within the novel. Lucian does indeed go mad, but there are long sections of the novel in which we can and probably will follow him into his madness, if only because his madness is art.

The artist is a dreamer. Even before he leaves for the London which will eventually destroy him, Lucian tends to inhabit the faun's world, literally seeing around him the erotically-charged and morally unhealthy splendors of Roman Caermaen rather than the prosaic provincialities that others see. These visions are products of imagination, and they are what make him an artist, yet they clearly make him fated to live beyond the compass of the social world. When Lucian, following his writer's destiny, makes the transition to London, he is no less haunted by the faun's vision. Because the faun has the power to see its world, not that of civilization, the overreaction of a woman he surprises in the fog makes him reach for "the stigmata of evil branding his forehead"[xviii] and hear her scream as "nocturnal Sabbath".[xix] And there are moments when London becomes:

> one grey temple of an awful rite, ring within
> ring of wizard stones crowded about some

> central place, every circle was an initiation,
> every initiation eternal loss.[xx]

The past is not merely objective history, but it also sleeps as memory and potential within the individual, accessible through imagination. The faun is a throwback to pagan Roman times, before the evolution of the moral sense had fostered and been fostered by Christianity.

The faun's other-focused vision, which we may more prosaically understand as the rather puritanical young man's compulsive and contradictory imagination, is connected with sexuality, and it is this which destroys him. In the final stages of the novel he becomes the lodger of a prostitute, but the delicately-raised young man who is not the faun cannot cope with the reality of this, and goes into what we now call denial. Thus by the end of the novel Lucian is a truly divided self: the faun, who like Hyde has always been really in charge, has led the boy into the faun's dwelling, and the boy has chosen madness and death rather than facing up to this.

Lucian is, in the exact, Aristotelean sense, a tragic hero. Much sympathy is invited for him, but so also is an understanding of his non-viability. Some have claimed otherwise, that he is more like Gissing's heroes, a noble, sacred spirit trapped in a disgustingly fallen world, but this reading is not in the end convincing. By the end of the tale we are clearly invited to see Lucian from outside, understanding much about him that he does not. But the best evidence to qualify the idea that Lucian can be seen as the champion of an unmediated aestheticism, an avatar of living in dreams, arises if we compare Lucian's life with that of his creator, Machen himself.

When the comparison is made, it quickly emerges that Lucian is Machen's vision of his own might-have-been – a turning in his life which he did not take. The early similarities between the biographies of writer and character are huge: both are born in Wales of a clergyman father, both are scholarly in temperament, both are unable to attend university, both move to London aided by a legacy, in quest of literature. Yet the similarities cease: Machen succeeded – and wanted to succeed - where Lucian failed.

It is possible that a further refinement of evolutionary theory prompted Machen to write this text in this form. In evolutionary theory, success is its own justification: when the white man invaded and the primitive inhabitant became extinct, this was seen merely as nature's way of clearing out anything unfit for life's great struggle. Lucian may be much lamented, but it was his creator who survived and by the late 1890s had a name, a wife, and a position in society.

We can't easily know exactly how Machen understood or evaluated his own avoidance of Lucian's fate. Did he see his escape as arising out of a difference in kind between him and his hero, or due only to a difference in degree? Did Machen sense himself as damned by the places his imagination caused him to visit? Publishers certainly did. Though it can be well-argued that the book is about the degenerate artist rather than itself an example of degeneracy, no publisher could be found when Machen finished writing the book, in 1897. Probably at that time only an entirely unsympathetic portrait of such an artist could have succeeded with the public. It was not until 1904, when the tide of backlash had receded considerably, that a magazine editor friend[xxi] dared to publish a truncated version, and the full text finally emerged as a book in 1907.[xxii]

In the post 1895 climate only the fittest aesthetes survived, and they did so by adapting. The Rhymers' Club disbanded: its minor poets faded away to premature death or suburban alcoholism while its one giant, W.B.Yeats, refined and transformed himself into someone else. The permissive periodicals, first *The Yellow Book* and then *The Savoy*, faded and died. Machen remained an artist of aesthete sensibility, yet his work changed in character in a way consonant with the threat that the aesthetes faced. In the period 1895 to 1899, as well as _The Hill of Dreams_, he wrote other texts that as much as anything in the period before 1895 can be considered decadent, aesthetic, engaged with terror-invoking sexuality. But there is evidence that Machen did sense himself as having a compromised imagination: increasingly, he turned aside from engaging with what we may call the pagan side of his imagination, which was where the trouble started, and instead developed something more 'spiritually wholesome', acceptable to a broader if less excitable public.

Thus, for example, very soon after _The Hill of Dreams_ he wrote "A Fragment of Life"[xxiii], a novella in which a married man of humble status (rather like H.G.Wells's Kipps or Mr Polly) finds his true spiritual destiny in the mystical worship of his forefathers and the landscapes of the Welsh valleys. This is fiction which has the power to move, but it lacks the rich ambiguity and complexity of vision which makes _The Hill of Dreams_ something more. At the turn of the century and in the years that followed, Machen was one of many who went on to purge and edit their earlier, racy aestheticism, until it became focused upon mysticism, which became a new watchword after 1900.

Machen himself, like other repentant aesthetes playing away from his older strengths, became progressively more interested in religion. He became champion of the ancient Celtic Church, of the religious faith of his ancestors, and of the reawakening of a potential for spiritual regeneration at the heart of materialism. At this point the wheel has come full circle: the beleaguered and threatened artist has fled back to his ancient pre-aesthete alliance, with the priesthood. This may seem something of a victory for the scientific culture which had been growing steadily in strength since the middle of the nineteenth century: science had identified itself with the voice of moral orthodoxy, had challenged the aesthete artist, and fought him to a standstill. But it was not all a victory for the scientists. The mysticism which the survivor-aesthetes adopted was one of the aspects of recent art which Nordau had fulminated upon. But the aesthetes no longer feared him when they had religion close at hand.

---

[i] I use 'artist' to designate all who work with imagination.

[ii] This idea goes back to Coleridge's view that "Imagination" has a special power, suggested in chapter 13 of his *Biographia Literaria*.

[iii] The periodical *The Yellow Book*, the medium by which so much decadent aesthetic art was visited upon the public, was edited by John Lane, the Bodley Head publisher, and ran from 1894 to 1897

[iv] Darwin's own vision is remarkably (thought not totally) free of the idea of upward or downward evolution. He emphasized only the very neutral idea of adaptation to environment.

[v] Thus for example, T.H.Huxley argued in *Evolution and Ethics* (1893) that humanity had benefited from two evolutionary processes, one as part of nature, one as part of culture.

[vi] Lombroso, Cesare, translated Havelock Ellis, *The Man of Genius*, London: Walter Scott, 1891.

[vii] Lombroso, op cit, pp 69-70.

[viii] Lombroso, op cit, pp 69-70

[ix] German *Entartung (1891)* published as *Degeneration*, London: William Heinemann, 1895.

[x] See chapter entitled "The Psychology of Mysticism", pp 46-66.

[xi] For a representative biography of Machen, see Valentine, Mark, *Arthur Machen*, Seren Books, 1995.

[xii] "The Great God Pan" first published in *The Great God Pan*, London: John Lane, 1895

[xiii] First in *St James Gazette* vol XXI, Sept 11, 1890, pp. 6-7. Available more recently in *Ritual and other stories*, Tartarus Press, 1992, pp35-38.

[xiv] Tales of Horror ad the Supernatural, London: The Richards Press, 1949, p 67.

[xv] Also first in *The Great God Pan*, London: John Lane, 1895.

[xvi] The Three Impostors, London: John Lane, pp 186-196.

---

xvii Written 1895-7, but, for reasons under discussion not published until 1904/1907.

xviii Fauns were horned.

xix *The Collected Arthur Machen*, London: Duckworth, 1988, p258.

xx ibid p 260.

xxi Published by A.E.Waite as "The Garden of Avallaunius" in *Horlicks Magazine*, July-December 1904.

xxii *The Hill of Dreams*, London: Grant Richards, 1907.

xxiii First in *Horlicks Magazine*, February-May, 1904.

# The Great God Pan

*Arthur Machen*

## The Experiment

**I** am glad you came, Clarke; very glad indeed. I was not sure
you could spare the time."

"I was able to make arrangements for a few days; things
are not very lively just now. But have you no misgivings,
Raymond? Is it absolutely safe?"

The two men were slowly pacing the terrace in front of Dr.
Raymond's house. The sun still hung above the western mountain-line,
but it shone with a dull red glow that cast no shadows, and all the air was
quiet; a sweet breath came from the great wood on the hillside above,
and with it, at intervals, the soft murmuring call of the wild doves.
Below, in the long lovely valley, the river wound in and out between the
lonely hills, and, as the sun hovered and vanished into the west, a faint
mist, pure white, began to rise from the hills. Dr. Raymond turned
sharply to his friend.

"Safe? Of course it is. In itself the operation is a perfectly simple one; any surgeon could do it."

"And there is no danger at any other stage?"

"None; absolutely no physical danger whatsoever, I give you my word. You are always timid, Clarke, always; but you know my history. I have devoted myself to transcendental medicine for the last twenty years. I have heard myself called quack and charlatan and impostor, but all the while I knew I was on the right path. Five years ago I reached the goal, and since then every day has been a preparation for what we shall do tonight."

"I should like to believe it is all true." Clarke knit his brows, and looked doubtfully at Dr. Raymond. "Are you perfectly sure, Raymond, that your theory is not a phantasmagoria—a splendid vision, certainly, but a mere vision after all?"

Dr. Raymond stopped in his walk and turned sharply. He was a middle-aged man, gaunt and thin, of a pale yellow complexion, but as he answered Clarke and faced him, there was a flush on his cheek.

"Look about you, Clarke. You see the mountain, and hill following after hill, as wave on wave, you see the woods and orchard, the fields of ripe corn, and the meadows reaching to the reed-beds by the river. You see me standing here beside you, and hear my voice; but I tell you that all these things— yes, from that star that has just shone out in the sky to the solid ground beneath our feet—I say that all these are but dreams and shadows; the shadows that hide the real world from our eyes. There is a real world, but it is beyond this glamour and this vision, beyond these 'chases in Arras, dreams in a career,' beyond them all as beyond a veil. I do not know whether any human being has ever lifted that veil; but I do know, Clarke, that you and I shall see it lifted this very night from before another's eyes. You may think this all strange nonsense; it may be strange, but it is true, and the ancients knew what lifting the veil means. They called it seeing the god Pan."

Clarke shivered; the white mist gathering over the river was chilly.

"It is wonderful indeed," he said. "We are standing on the brink of a strange world, Raymond, if what you say is true. I suppose the knife is absolutely necessary?"

"Yes; a slight lesion in the grey matter, that is all; a trifling rearrangement of certain cells, a microscopical alteration that would escape the attention of ninety-nine brain specialists out of a hundred. I don't want to bother you with 'shop,' Clarke; I might give you a mass of technical detail which would sound very imposing, and would leave you as enlightened as you are now. But I suppose you have read, casually, in out-of-the-way corners of your paper, that immense strides have been made recently in the physiology of the brain. I saw a paragraph the other day about Digby's theory, and Browne Faber's discoveries. Theories and discoveries! Where they are standing now, I stood fifteen years ago, and I need not tell you that I have not been standing still for the last fifteen years. It will be enough if I say that five years ago I made the discovery that I alluded to when I said that ten years ago I reached the goal. After years of labour, after years of toiling and groping in the dark, after days and nights of disappointments and sometimes of despair, in which I used now and then to tremble and grow cold with the thought that perhaps there were others seeking for what I sought, at last, after so long, a pang of sudden joy thrilled my soul, and I knew the long journey was at an end. By what seemed then and still seems a chance, the suggestion of a moment's idle thought followed up upon familiar lines and paths that I had tracked a hundred times already, the great truth burst upon me, and I saw, mapped out in lines of sight, a whole world, a sphere unknown; continents and islands, and great oceans in which no ship has sailed (to my belief) since a Man first lifted up his eyes and beheld the sun, and the stars of heaven, and the quiet earth beneath. You will think this all high-flown language, Clarke, but it is hard to be literal. And yet; I do not know whether what I am hinting at cannot be set forth in plain and lonely terms. For instance, this world of ours is pretty well girded now with the telegraph wires and cables; thought, with something less than the speed of thought, flashes from sunrise to sunset, from north to south, across the floods and the desert places. Suppose that an electrician of today were suddenly to perceive that he and his friends have merely been playing with pebbles and mistaking them for the foundations of the world; suppose that such a man saw uttermost space lie open before the current, and words of men flash forth to the sun and beyond the sun into the systems beyond, and the voice of articulate-speaking men echo in the waste void that bounds our thought. As analogies go, that is a pretty good analogy of what I have done; you can understand now a little of what I felt as I stood here one evening; it was a summer evening, and the valley looked much as it does now; I stood here, and saw before me the unutterable, the unthinkable gulf that yawns profound between two worlds, the world of matter and the world of spirit; I saw the great empty deep stretch dim before me, and in that instant a bridge of light leapt from the earth to the unknown shore, and the abyss was spanned. You may look in Browne Faber's book, if you like, and you will find that to the present day men of science are unable to account for the presence, or to specify the functions of a certain group of nerve-cells in the brain. That group is, as it were, land to let, a mere waste place for fanciful theories. I am not in the position of Browne Faber and the specialists, I am perfectly instructed as to the possible functions of those nerve-centers in the scheme of things. With a touch I can bring them into play, with a touch, I say, I can set free the current, with a touch I can complete the communication between this world of sense and—we shall be able to finish the sentence later on. Yes, the knife is necessary; but think what that knife will effect. It will level utterly the solid wall of sense, and probably, for the first time since man was made, a spirit will gaze on a spirit-world. Clarke, Mary will see the god Pan!"

"But you remember what you wrote to me? I thought it would be requisite that she—"

He whispered the rest into the doctor's ear.

"Not at all, not at all. That is nonsense. I assure you. Indeed, it is better as it is; I am quite certain of that."

"Consider the matter well, Raymond. It's a great responsibility. Something might go wrong; you would be a miserable man for the rest of your days."

"No, I think not, even if the worst happened. As you know, I rescued Mary from the gutter, and from almost certain starvation, when she was a child; I think her life is mine, to use as I see fit. Come, it's getting late; we had better go in."

Dr. Raymond led the way into the house, through the hall, and down a long dark passage. He took a key from his pocket and opened a heavy door, and motioned Clarke into his laboratory. It had once been a billiard-room, and was lighted by a glass dome in the centre of the ceiling, whence there still shone a sad grey light on the figure of the doctor as he lit a lamp with a heavy shade and placed it on a table in the middle of the room.

Clarke looked about him. Scarcely a foot of wall remained bare; there were shelves all around laden with bottles and phials of all shapes and colours, and at one end stood a little Chippendale book-case. Raymond pointed to this.

"You see that parchment Oswald Crollius? He was one of the first to show me the way, though I don't think he ever found it himself. That is a strange saying of his: 'In every grain of wheat there lies hidden the soul of a star.'"

There was not much furniture in the laboratory. The table in the centre, a stone slab with a drain in one corner, the two armchairs on which Raymond and Clarke were sitting; that was all, except an odd-looking chair at the furthest end of the room. Clarke looked at it, and raised his eyebrows.

"Yes, that is the chair," said Raymond. "We may as well place it in position." He got up and wheeled the chair to the light, and began raising and lowering it, letting down the seat, setting the back at various angles, and adjusting the foot-rest. It looked comfortable enough, and Clarke passed his hand over the soft green velvet, as the doctor manipulated the levers.

"Now, Clarke, make yourself quite comfortable. I have a couple hours' work before me; I was obliged to leave certain matters to the last."

Raymond went to the stone slab, and Clarke watched him drearily as he bent over a row of phials and lit the flame under the crucible. The doctor had a small hand-lamp, shaded as the larger one, on a ledge above his apparatus, and Clarke, who sat in the shadows, looked down at the great shadowy room, wondering at the bizarre effects of brilliant light and undefined darkness contrasting with one another. Soon he became conscious of an odd odour, at first the merest suggestion of odour, in the room, and as it grew more decided he felt surprised that he was not reminded of the chemist's shop or the surgery. Clarke found himself idly endeavouring to analyse the sensation, and half conscious, he began to think of a day, fifteen years ago, that he had spent roaming through the woods and meadows near his own home. It was a burning day at the beginning of August, the heat had dimmed the outlines of all things and all distances with a faint mist, and people who observed the thermometer spoke of an abnormal register, of a temperature that was almost tropical. Strangely that wonderful hot day of the fifties rose up again in Clarke's imagination; the sense of dazzling all-pervading sunlight seemed to blot out the shadows and the lights of the laboratory, and he felt again the heated air beating in gusts about his face, saw the shimmer rising from the turf, and heard the myriad murmur of the summer.

"I hope the smell doesn't annoy you, Clarke; there's nothing unwholesome about it. It may make you a bit sleepy, that's all."

Clarke heard the words quite distinctly, and knew that Raymond was speaking to him, but for the life of him he could not rouse himself from his lethargy. He could only think of the lonely walk he had taken fifteen years ago; it was his last look at the fields and woods he had known since he was a child, and now it all stood out in brilliant light, as a picture, before him. Above all there came to his nostrils the scent of summer, the smell of flowers mingled, and the odour of the woods, of cool shaded places, deep in the green depths, drawn forth by the sun's heat; and the scent of the good earth, lying as it were with arms stretched forth, and smiling lips, overpowered all. His fancies made him wander, as he had wandered long ago, from the fields into the wood, tracking a little path between the shining undergrowth of beech-trees; and the trickle of water dropping from the limestone rock sounded as a clear melody in the dream. Thoughts began to go astray and to mingle with other thoughts; the beech alley was transformed to a path between ilex-trees, and here and there a vine climbed from bough to bough, and sent up waving tendrils and drooped with purple grapes, and the sparse grey-green leaves of a wild olive-tree stood out against the dark shadows of the ilex. Clarke, in the deep folds of dream, was conscious that the path from his father's house had led him into an undiscovered country, and he was wondering at the strangeness of it all, when suddenly, in place of the hum and murmur of the summer, an infinite silence seemed to fall on all things, and the wood was hushed, and for a moment in time he stood face to face there with a presence, that was neither man nor beast, neither the living nor the dead, but all things mingled, the form of all things but devoid of all form. And in that moment, the sacrament of body and soul was dissolved, and a voice seemed to cry "Let us go hence," and then the darkness of darkness beyond the stars, the darkness of everlasting.

When Clarke woke up with a start he saw Raymond pouring a few drops of some oily fluid into a green phial, which he stoppered tightly.

"You have been dozing," he said; "the journey must have tired you out. It is done now. I am going to fetch Mary; I shall be back in ten minutes."

Clarke lay back in his chair and wondered. It seemed as if he had but passed from one dream into another. He half expected to see the walls of the laboratory melt and disappear, and to awake in London, shuddering at his own sleeping fancies. But at last the door opened, and the doctor returned, and behind him came a girl of about seventeen, dressed all in white. She was so beautiful that Clarke did not wonder at what the doctor had written to him. She was blushing now over face and neck and arms, but Raymond seemed unmoved.

"Mary," he said, "the time has come. You are quite free. Are you willing to trust yourself to me entirely?"

"Yes, dear."

"Do you hear that, Clarke? You are my witness. Here is the chair, Mary. It is quite easy. Just sit in it and lean back. Are you ready?"

"Yes, dear, quite ready. Give me a kiss before you begin."

The doctor stooped and kissed her mouth, kindly enough. "Now shut your eyes," he said. The girl closed her eyelids, as if she were tired, and longed for sleep, and Raymond placed the green phial to her nostrils. Her face grew white, whiter than her dress; she struggled faintly, and then with the feeling of submission strong within her, crossed her arms upon her breast as a little child about to say her prayers. The bright light of the lamp fell full upon her, and Clarke watched changes fleeting over her face as the changes of the hills when the summer clouds float across the sun. And then she lay all white and still, and the doctor turned up one of her eyelids. She was quite unconscious. Raymond pressed hard on one of the levers and the chair instantly sank back. Clarke saw him cutting away a circle, like a tonsure, from her hair, and the lamp was moved nearer. Raymond took a small glittering instrument from a little case, and Clarke turned away shudderingly. When he looked again the doctor was binding up the wound he had made.

"She will awake in five minutes." Raymond was still perfectly cool. "There is nothing more to be done; we can only wait."

The minutes passed slowly; they could hear a slow, heavy, ticking. There was an old clock in the passage. Clarke felt sick and faint; his knees shook beneath him, he could hardly stand.

Suddenly, as they watched, they heard a long-drawn sigh, and suddenly did the colour that had vanished return to the girl's cheeks, and suddenly her eyes opened. Clarke quailed before them. They shone with an awful light, looking far away, and a great wonder fell upon her face, and her hands stretched out as if to touch what was invisible; but in an instant the wonder faded, and gave place to the most awful terror. The muscles of her face were hideously convulsed, she shook from head to foot; the soul seemed struggling and shuddering within the house of flesh. It was a horrible sight, and Clarke rushed forward, as she fell shrieking to the floor.

Three days later Raymond took Clarke to Mary's bedside. She was lying wide-awake, rolling her head from side to side, and grinning vacantly.

"Yes," said the doctor, still quite cool, "it is a great pity; she is a hopeless idiot. However, it could not be helped; and, after all, she has seen the Great God Pan."

## Mr. Clarke's Memoirs

Mr. Clarke, the gentleman chosen by Dr. Raymond to witness the strange experiment of the god Pan, was a person in whose character caution and curiosity were oddly mingled; in his sober moments he thought of the unusual and eccentric with undisguised aversion, and yet, deep in his heart, there was a wide-eyed inquisitiveness with respect to all the more recondite and esoteric elements in the nature of men. The latter tendency had prevailed when he accepted Raymond's invitation, for though his considered judgment had always repudiated the doctor's theories as the wildest nonsense, yet he secretly hugged a belief in fantasy, and would have rejoiced to see that belief confirmed. The horrors that he witnessed in the dreary laboratory were to a certain extent salutary; he was conscious of being involved in an affair not altogether reputable, and for many years afterwards he clung bravely to the commonplace, and rejected all occasions of occult investigation. Indeed, on some homeopathic principle, he for some time attended the seances of distinguished mediums, hoping that the clumsy tricks of these gentlemen would make him altogether disgusted with mysticism of every kind, but the remedy, though caustic, was not efficacious. Clarke knew that he still pined for the unseen, and little by little, the old passion began to reassert itself, as the face of Mary, shuddering and convulsed with an unknown terror, faded slowly from his memory. Occupied all day in pursuits both serious and lucrative, the temptation to relax in the evening was too great, especially in the winter months, when the fire cast a warm glow over his snug bachelor apartment, and a bottle of some choice claret stood ready by his elbow. His dinner digested, he would make a brief pretence of reading the evening paper, but the mere catalogue of news soon palled upon him, and Clarke would find himself casting glances of warm desire in the direction of an old Japanese bureau, which stood at a pleasant distance from the hearth. Like a boy before a jam-closet, for a few minutes he would hover indecisive, but lust always prevailed, and Clarke ended by drawing up his chair, lighting a candle, and sitting down before the bureau. Its pigeon-holes and drawers teemed with documents on the most morbid subjects, and in the well reposed a large manuscript volume, in which he had painfully entered he gems of his collection. Clarke had a fine contempt for published literature; the most ghostly story ceased to interest him if it happened to be printed; his sole pleasure was in the reading, compiling, and rearranging what he called his "Memoirs to prove the Existence of the Devil," and engaged in this pursuit the evening seemed to fly and the night appeared too short.

On one particular evening, an ugly December night, black with fog, and raw with frost, Clarke hurried over his dinner, and scarcely deigned to observe his customary ritual of taking up the paper and laying it down again. He paced two or three times up and down the room, and opened the bureau, stood still a moment, and sat down. He leant back, absorbed in one of those dreams to which he was subject, and at length drew out his book, and opened it at the last entry. There were three or four pages densely covered with Clarke's round, set penmanship, and at the beginning he had written in a somewhat larger hand:

Singular Narrative told me by my Friend, Dr. Phillips. He assures me that all the facts related therein are strictly and wholly True, but refuses to give either the Surnames of the Persons Concerned, or the Place where these Extraordinary Events occurred.

Mr. Clarke began to read over the account for the tenth time, glancing now and then at the pencil notes he had made when it was told him by his friend. It was one of his humours to pride himself on a certain literary ability; he thought well of his style, and took pains in arranging the circumstances in dramatic order. He read the following story:—

The persons concerned in this statement are Helen V., who, if she is still alive, must now be a woman of twenty-three, Rachel M., since deceased, who was a year younger than the above, and Trevor W., an imbecile, aged eighteen. These persons were at the period of the story inhabitants of a village on the borders of Wales, a place of some importance in the time of the Roman occupation, but now a scattered hamlet, of not more than five hundred souls. It is situated on rising ground, about six miles from the sea, and is sheltered by a large and picturesque forest.

Some eleven years ago, Helen V. came to the village under rather peculiar circumstances. It is understood that she, being an orphan, was adopted in her infancy by a distant relative, who brought her up in his own house until she was twelve years old. Thinking, however, that it would be better for the child to have playmates of her own age, he advertised in several local papers for a good home in a comfortable farmhouse for a girl of twelve, and this advertisement was answered by Mr. R., a well-to-do farmer in the above-mentioned village. His references proving satisfactory, the gentleman sent his adopted daughter to Mr. R., with a letter, in which he stipulated that the girl should have a room to herself, and stated that her guardians need be at no trouble in the matter of education, as she was already sufficiently educated for the position in life which she would occupy. In fact, Mr. R. was given to understand that the girl be allowed to find her own occupations and to spend her time almost as she liked. Mr. R. duly met her at the nearest station, a town seven miles away from his house, and seems to have remarked nothing extraordinary about the child except that she was reticent as to her former life and her adopted father. She was, however, of a very different type from the inhabitants of the village; her skin was a pale, clear olive, and her features were strongly marked, and of a somewhat foreign character. She appears to have settled down easily enough into farmhouse life, and became a favourite with the children, who sometimes went with her on her rambles in the forest, for this was her amusement. Mr. R. states that he has known her to go out by herself directly after their early breakfast, and not return till after dusk, and that, feeling uneasy at a young girl being out alone for so many hours, he communicated with her adopted father, who replied in a brief note that Helen must do as she chose. In the winter, when the forest paths are impassable, she spent most of her time in her bedroom, where she slept alone, according to the instructions of her relative. It was on one of these expeditions to the forest that the first of the singular incidents with which this girl is connected occurred, the date being about a year after her arrival at the village. The preceding winter had been remarkably severe, the snow drifting to a great depth, and the frost continuing for an unexampled period, and the summer following was as noteworthy for its extreme heat. On one of the very hottest days in this summer, Helen V. left the farmhouse for one of her long rambles in the forest, taking with her, as usual, some bread and meat for lunch. She was seen by some men in the fields making for the old Roman Road, a green causeway which traverses the highest part of the wood, and they were astonished to observe that the girl had taken off her hat, though the heat of the sun was already tropical. As it happened, a labourer, Joseph W. by name, was working in the forest near the Roman Road, and at twelve o'clock his little son, Trevor, brought the man his dinner of bread and cheese. After the meal, the boy, who was about seven years old at the time, left his father at work, and, as he said, went to look for flowers in the wood, and the man, who could hear him shouting with delight at his discoveries, felt no uneasiness. Suddenly, however, he was horrified at hearing the most dreadful screams, evidently the result of great terror, proceeding from the direction in which his son had gone, and he hastily threw down his tools and ran to see what had happened. Tracing his path by the sound, he met the little boy, who was running headlong, and was evidently terribly frightened, and on questioning him the man elicited that after picking a posy of flowers he felt tired, and lay down on the grass and fell asleep. He was suddenly awakened, as he stated, by a peculiar noise, a sort of singing he called it, and on peeping through the branches he saw Helen V. playing on the grass with a "strange naked man," who he seemed unable to describe more fully. He said he felt dreadfully frightened and ran away crying for his father. Joseph W. proceeded in the direction indicated by his son, and found Helen V. sitting on the grass in the middle of a glade or open space left by charcoal burners. He angrily charged her with frightening his little boy, but she entirely denied the accusation and laughed at the child's story of a "strange man," to which he himself did not attach much credence. Joseph W. came to the conclusion that the boy had woke up with a sudden fright, as children sometimes do, but Trevor persisted in his story, and continued in such evident distress that at last his father took him home, hoping that his mother would be able to soothe him. For many weeks, however, the boy gave his parents much anxiety; he became nervous and strange in his manner, refusing to leave the cottage by himself, and constantly alarming the household by waking in the night with cries of "The man in the wood! father! father!"

In course of time, however, the impression seemed to have worn off, and about three months later he accompanied his father to the home of a gentleman in the neighborhood, for whom Joseph W. occasionally did work. The man was shown into the study, and the little boy was left sitting in the hall, and a few minutes later, while the gentleman was giving W. his instructions, they were both horrified by a piercing shriek and the sound of a fall, and rushing out they found the child lying senseless on the floor, his face contorted with terror. The doctor was immediately summoned, and after some examination he pronounced the child to be suffering form a kind of fit, apparently produced by a sudden shock. The boy was taken to one of the bedrooms, and after some time recovered consciousness, but only to pass into a condition described by the medical man as one of violent hysteria. The doctor exhibited a strong sedative, and in the course of two hours pronounced him fit to walk home, but in passing through the hall the paroxysms of fright returned and with additional violence. The father perceived that the child was pointing at some object, and heard the old cry, "The man in the wood," and looking in the direction indicated saw a stone head of grotesque appearance, which had been built into the wall above one of the doors. It seems the owner of the house had recently made alterations in his premises, and on digging the foundations for some offices, the men had found a curious head, evidently of the Roman period, which had been placed in the manner described. The head is pronounced by the most experienced archaeologists of the district to be that of a faun or satyr. (Dr. Phillips tells me that he has seen the head in question, and assures me that he has never received such a vivid presentment of intense evil.)

From whatever cause arising, this second shock seemed too severe for the boy Trevor, and at the present date he suffers from a weakness of intellect, which gives but little promise of amending. The matter caused a good deal of sensation at the time, and the girl Helen was closely questioned by Mr. R., but to no purpose, she steadfastly denying that she had frightened or in any way molested Trevor.

The second event with which this girl's name is connected took place about six years ago, and is of a still more extraordinary character.

At the beginning of the summer of 1882, Helen contracted a friendship of a peculiarly intimate character with Rachel M., the daughter of a prosperous farmer in the neighbourhood. This girl, who was a year younger than Helen, was considered by most people to be the prettier of the two, though Helen's features had to a great extent softened as she became older. The two girls, who were together on every available opportunity, presented a singular contrast, the one with her clear, olive skin and almost Italian appearance, and the other of the proverbial red and white of our rural districts. It must be stated that the payments made to Mr. R. for the maintenance of Helen were known in the village for their excessive liberality, and the impression was general that she would one day inherit a large sum of money from her relative. The parents of Rachel were therefore not averse from their daughter's friendship with the girl, and even encouraged the intimacy, though they now bitterly regret having done so. Helen still retained her extraordinary fondness for the forest, and on several occasions Rachel accompanied her, the two friends setting out early in the morning, and remaining in the wood until dusk. Once or twice after these excursions Mrs. M. thought her daughter's manner rather peculiar; she seemed languid and dreamy, and as it has been expressed, "different from herself," but these peculiarities seem to have been thought too trifling for remark. One evening, however, after Rachel had come home, her mother heard a noise which sounded like suppressed weeping in the girl's room, and on going in found her lying, half undressed, upon the bed, evidently in the greatest distress. As soon as she saw her mother, she exclaimed, "Ah, mother, mother, why did you let me go to the forest with Helen?" Mrs. M. was astonished at so strange a question, and proceeded to make inquiries. Rachel told her a wild story. She said—

Clarke closed the book with a snap, and turned his chair towards the fire. When his friend sat one evening in that very chair, and told his story, Clarke had interrupted him at a point a little subsequent to this, had cut short his words in a paroxysm of horror. "My God!" he had exclaimed, "think, think what you are saying. It is too incredible, too monstrous; such things can never be in this quiet world, where men and women live and die, and struggle, and conquer, or maybe fail, and fall down under sorrow, and grieve and suffer strange fortunes for many a year; but not this, Phillips, not such things as this. There must be some explanation, some way out of the terror. Why, man, if such a case were possible, our earth would be a nightmare."

But Phillips had told his story to the end, concluding:

"Her flight remains a mystery to this day; she vanished in broad sunlight; they saw her walking in a meadow, and a few moments later she was not there."

Clarke tried to conceive the thing again, as he sat by the fire, and again his mind shuddered and shrank back, appalled before the sight of such awful, unspeakable elements enthroned as it were, and triumphant in human flesh. Before him stretched the long dim vista of the green causeway in the forest, as his friend had described it; he saw the swaying leaves and the quivering shadows on the grass, he saw the sunlight and the flowers, and far away, far in the long distance, the two figure moved toward him. One was Rachel, but the other?

Clarke had tried his best to disbelieve it all, but at the end of the account, as he had written it in his book, he had placed the inscription:

ET DIABOLVS INCARNATE EST. ET HOMO FACTVS EST.

## The City Of Resurrections

"Herbert! Good God! Is it possible?"

"Yes, my name's Herbert. I think I know your face, too, but I don't remember your name. My memory is very queer."

"Don't you recollect Villiers of Wadham?"

"So it is, so it is. I beg your pardon, Villiers, I didn't think I was begging of an old college friend. Good-night."

"My dear fellow, this haste is unnecessary. My rooms are close by, but we won't go there just yet. Suppose we walk up Shaftesbury Avenue a little way? But how in heaven's name have you come to this pass, Herbert?"

"It's a long story, Villiers, and a strange one too, but you can hear it if you like."

"Come on, then. Take my arm, you don't seem very strong."

The ill-assorted pair moved slowly up Rupert Street; the one in dirty, evil-looking rags, and the other attired in the regulation uniform of a man about town, trim, glossy, and eminently well-to-do. Villiers had emerged from his restaurant after an excellent dinner of many courses, assisted by an ingratiating little flask of Chianti, and, in that frame of mind which was with him almost chronic, had delayed a moment by the door, peering round in the dimly-lighted street in search of those mysterious incidents and persons with which the streets of London teem in every quarter and every hour. Villiers prided himself as a practised explorer of such obscure mazes and byways of London life, and in this unprofitable pursuit he displayed an assiduity which was worthy of more serious employment. Thus he stood by the lamp-post surveying the passers-by with undisguised curiosity, and with that gravity known only to the systematic diner, had just enunciated in his mind the formula: "London has been called the city of encounters; it is more than that, it is the city of Resurrections," when these reflections were suddenly interrupted by a piteous whine at his elbow, and a deplorable appeal for alms. He looked around in some irritation, and with a sudden shock found himself confronted with the embodied proof of his somewhat stilted fancies. There, close beside him, his face altered and disfigured by poverty and disgrace, his body barely covered by greasy ill-fitting rags, stood his old friend Charles Herbert, who had matriculated on the same day as himself, with whom he had been merry and wise for twelve revolving terms. Different occupations and varying interests had interrupted the friendship, and it was six years since Villiers had seen Herbert; and now he looked upon this wreck of a man with grief and dismay, mingled with a certain inquisitiveness as to what dreary chain of circumstances had dragged him down to such a doleful pass. Villiers felt together with compassion all the relish of the amateur in mysteries, and congratulated himself on his leisurely speculations outside the restaurant.

They walked on in silence for some time, and more than one passer-by stared in astonishment at the unaccustomed spectacle of a well-dressed man with an unmistakable beggar hanging on to his arm, and, observing this, Villiers led the way to an obscure street in Soho. Here he repeated his question.

"How on earth has it happened, Herbert? I always understood you would succeed to an excellent position in Dorsetshire. Did your father disinherit you? Surely not?"

"No, Villiers; I came into all the property at my poor father's death; he died a year after I left Oxford. He was a very good father to me, and I mourned his death sincerely enough. But you know what young men are; a few months later I came up to town and went a good deal into society. Of course I had excellent introductions, and I managed to enjoy myself very much in a harmless sort of way. I played a little, certainly, but never for heavy stakes, and the few bets I made on races brought me in money—only a few pounds, you know, but enough to pay for cigars and such petty pleasures. It was in my second season that the tide turned. Of course you have heard of my marriage?"

"No, I never heard anything about it."

"Yes, I married, Villiers. I met a girl, a girl of the most wonderful and most strange beauty, at the house of some people whom I knew. I cannot tell you her age; I never knew it, but, so far as I can guess, I should think she must have been about nineteen when I made her acquaintance. My friends had come to know her at Florence; she told them she was an orphan, the child of an English father and an Italian mother, and she charmed them as she charmed me. The first time I saw her was at an evening party. I was standing by the door talking to a friend, when suddenly above the hum and babble of conversation I heard a voice which seemed to thrill to my heart. She was singing an Italian song. I was introduced to her that evening, and in three months I married Helen. Villiers, that woman, if I can call her woman, corrupted my soul. The night of the wedding I found myself sitting in her bedroom in the hotel, listening to her talk. She was sitting up in bed, and I listened to her as she spoke in her beautiful voice, spoke of things which even now I would not dare whisper in the blackest night, though I stood in the midst of a wilderness. You, Villiers, you may think you know life, and London, and what goes on day and night in this dreadful city; for all I can say you may have heard the talk of the vilest, but I tell you you can have no conception of what I know, not in your most fantastic, hideous dreams can you have imaged forth the faintest shadow of what I have heard—and seen. Yes, seen. I have seen the incredible, such horrors that even I myself sometimes stop in the middle of the street and ask whether it is possible for a man to behold such things and live. In a year, Villiers, I was a ruined man, in body and soul—in body and soul."

"But your property, Herbert? You had land in Dorset."

"I sold it all; the fields and woods, the dear old house—everything."

"And the money?"

"She took it all from me."

"And then left you?"

"Yes; she disappeared one night. I don't know where she went, but I am sure if I saw her again it would kill me. The rest of my story is of no interest; sordid misery, that is all. You may think, Villiers, that I have exaggerated and talked for effect; but I have not told you half. I could tell you certain things which would convince you, but you would never know a happy day again. You would pass the rest of your life, as I pass mine, a haunted man, a man who has seen hell."

Villiers took the unfortunate man to his rooms, and gave him a meal. Herbert could eat little, and scarcely touched the glass of wine set before him. He sat moody and silent by the fire, and seemed relieved when Villiers sent him away with a small present of money.

"By the way, Herbert," said Villiers, as they parted at the door, "what was your wife's name? You said Helen, I think? Helen what?"

"The name she passed under when I met her was Helen Vaughan, but what her real name was I can't say. I don't think she had a name. No, no, not in that sense. Only human beings have names, Villiers; I can't say anymore. Good-bye; yes, I will not fail to call if I see any way in which you can help me. Good-night."

The man went out into the bitter night, and Villiers returned to his fireside. There was something about Herbert which shocked him inexpressibly; not his poor rags nor the marks which poverty had set upon his face, but rather an indefinite terror which hung about him like a mist. He had acknowledged that he himself was not devoid of blame; the woman, he had avowed, had corrupted him body and soul, and Villiers felt that this man, once his friend, had been an actor in scenes evil beyond the power of words. His story needed no confirmation: he himself was the embodied proof of it. Villiers mused curiously over the story he had heard, and wondered whether he had heard both the first and the last of it. "No," he thought, "certainly not the last, probably only the beginning. A case like this is like a nest of Chinese boxes; you open one after the other and find a quainter workmanship in every box. Most likely poor Herbert is merely one of the outside boxes; there are stranger ones to follow."

Villiers could not take his mind away from Herbert and his story, which seemed to grow wilder as the night wore on. The fire seemed to burn low, and the chilly air of the morning crept into the room; Villiers got up with a glance over his shoulder, and, shivering slightly, went to bed.

A few days later he saw at his club a gentleman of his acquaintance, named Austin, who was famous for his intimate knowledge of London life, both in its tenebrous and luminous phases. Villiers, still full of his encounter in Soho and its consequences, thought Austin might possibly be able to shed some light on Herbert's history, and so after some casual talk he suddenly put the question:

"Do you happen to know anything of a man named Herbert — Charles Herbert?"

Austin turned round sharply and stared at Villiers with some astonishment.

"Charles Herbert? Weren't you in town three years ago? No; then you have not heard of the Paul Street case? It caused a good deal of sensation at the time."

"What was the case?"

"Well, a gentleman, a man of very good position, was found dead, stark dead, in the area of a certain house in Paul Street, off Tottenham Court Road. Of course the police did not make the discovery; if you happen to be sitting up all night and have a light in your window, the constable will ring the bell, but if you happen to be lying dead in somebody's area, you will be left alone. In this instance, as in many others, the alarm was raised by some kind of vagabond; I don't mean a common tramp, or a public-house loafer, but a gentleman, whose business or pleasure, or both, made him a spectator of the London streets at five o'clock in the morning. This individual was, as he said, 'going home,' it did not appear whence or whither, and had occasion to pass through Paul Street between four and five a.m. Something or other caught his eye at Number 20; he said, absurdly enough, that the house had the most unpleasant physiognomy he had ever observed, but, at any rate, he glanced down the area and was a good deal astonished to see a man lying on the stones, his limbs all huddled together, and his face turned up. Our gentleman thought his face looked peculiarly ghastly, and so set off at a run in search of the nearest policeman. The constable was at first inclined to treat the matter lightly, suspecting common drunkenness; however, he came, and after looking at the man's face, changed his tone, quickly enough. The early bird, who had picked up this fine worm, was sent off for a doctor, and the policeman rang and knocked at the door till a slatternly servant girl came down looking more than half asleep. The constable pointed out the contents of the area to the maid, who screamed loudly enough to wake up the street, but she knew nothing of the man; had never seen him at the house, and so forth. Meanwhile, the original discoverer had come back with a medical man, and the next thing was to get into the area. The gate was open, so the whole quartet stumped down the steps. The doctor hardly needed a moment's examination; he said the poor fellow had been dead for several hours, and it was then the case began to get interesting. The dead man had not been robbed, and in one of his pockets were papers identifying him as—well, as a man of good family and means, a favourite in society, and nobody's enemy, as far as could be known. I don't give his name, Villiers, because it has nothing to do with the story, and because it's no good raking up these affairs about the dead when there are no relations living. The next curious point was that the medical men couldn't agree as to how he met his death. There were some slight bruises on his shoulders, but they were so slight that it looked as if he had been pushed roughly out of the kitchen door, and not thrown over the railings from the street or even dragged down the steps. But there were positively no other marks of violence about him, certainly none that would account for his death; and when they came to the autopsy there wasn't a trace of poison of any kind. Of course the police wanted to know all about the people at Number 20, and here again, so I have heard from private sources, one or two other very curious points came out. It appears that the occupants of the house were a Mr. and Mrs. Charles Herbert; he was said to be a landed proprietor, though it struck most people that Paul Street was not exactly the place to look for country gentry. As for Mrs. Herbert, nobody seemed to know who or what she was, and, between ourselves, I fancy the divers after her history found themselves in rather strange waters. Of course they both denied knowing anything about the deceased, and in default of any evidence against them they were discharged. But some very odd things came out about them. Though it was between five and six in the morning when the dead man was removed, a large crowd had collected, and several of the neighbours ran to see what was going on. They were pretty free with their comments, by all accounts, and from these it appeared that Number 20 was in very bad odour in Paul Street. The detectives tried to trace down these rumours to some solid foundation of fact, but could not get hold of anything. People shook their heads and raised their eyebrows and thought the Herberts rather 'queer,' 'would rather not be seen going into their house,' and so on, but there was nothing tangible. The authorities were morally certain the man met his death in some way or another in the house and was thrown out by the kitchen door, but they couldn't prove it, and the absence of any indications of violence or poisoning left them helpless. An odd case, wasn't it? But curiously enough, there's something more that I haven't told you. I happened to know one of the doctors who was consulted as to the cause of death, and some time after the inquest I met him, and asked him about it. 'Do you really mean to tell me,' I said, 'that you were baffled by the case, that you actually don't know what the man died of?' 'Pardon me,' he replied, 'I know perfectly well what caused death. Blank died of fright, of sheer, awful terror; I never saw features so hideously contorted in the entire course of my practice, and I have seen the faces of a whole host of dead.' The doctor was usually a cool customer enough, and a certain vehemence in his manner struck me, but I couldn't get anything more out of him. I suppose the Treasury didn't see their way to prosecuting the Herberts for frightening a man to death; at any rate, nothing was done, and the case dropped out of men's minds. Do you happen to know anything of Herbert?"

"Well," replied Villiers, "he was an old college friend of mine."

"You don't say so? Have you ever seen his wife?"

"No, I haven't. I have lost sight of Herbert for many years."

"It's queer, isn't it, parting with a man at the college gate or at Paddington, seeing nothing of him for years, and then finding him pop up his head in such an odd place. But I should like to have seen Mrs. Herbert; people said extraordinary things about her."

"What sort of things?"

"Well, I hardly know how to tell you. Everyone who saw her at the police court said she was at once the most beautiful woman and the most repulsive they had ever set eyes on. I have spoken to a man who saw her, and I assure you he positively shuddered as he tried to describe the woman, but he couldn't tell why. She seems to have been a sort of enigma; and I expect if that one dead man could have told tales, he would have told some uncommonly queer ones. And there you are again in another puzzle; what could a respectable country gentleman like Mr. Blank (we'll call him that if you don't mind) want in such a very queer house as Number 20? It's altogether a very odd case, isn't it?"

"It is indeed, Austin; an extraordinary case. I didn't think, when I asked you about my old friend, I should strike on such strange metal. Well, I must be off; good-day."

Villiers went away, thinking of his own conceit of the Chinese boxes; here was quaint workmanship indeed.

## The Discovery In Paul Street

A few months after Villiers' meeting with Herbert, Mr. Clarke was sitting, as usual, by his after-dinner hearth, resolutely guarding his fancies from wandering in the direction of the bureau. For more than a week he had succeeded in keeping away from the "Memoirs," and he cherished hopes of a complete self-reformation; but, in spite of his endeavours, he could not hush the wonder and the strange curiosity that the last case he had written down had excited within him. He had put the case, or rather the outline of it, conjecturally to a scientific friend, who shook his head, and thought Clarke getting queer, and on this particular evening Clarke was making an effort to rationalize the story, when a sudden knock at the door roused him from his meditations.

"Mr. Villiers to see you sir."

"Dear me, Villiers, it is very kind of you to look me up; I have not seen you for many months; I should think nearly a year. Come in, come in. And how are you, Villiers? Want any advice about investments?"

"No, thanks, I fancy everything I have in that way is pretty safe. No, Clarke, I have really come to consult you about a rather curious matter that has been brought under my notice of late. I am afraid you will think it all rather absurd when I tell my tale. I sometimes think so myself, and that's just what I made up my mind to come to you, as I know you're a practical man."

Mr. Villiers was ignorant of the "Memoirs to prove the Existence of the Devil."

"Well, Villiers, I shall be happy to give you my advice, to the best of my ability. What is the nature of the case?"

"It's an extraordinary thing altogether. You know my ways; I always keep my eyes open in the streets, and in my time I have chanced upon some queer customers, and queer cases too, but this, I think, beats all. I was coming out of a restaurant one nasty winter night about three months ago; I had had a capital dinner and a good bottle of Chianti, and I stood for a moment on the pavement, thinking what a mystery there is about London streets and the companies that pass along them. A bottle of red wine encourages these fancies, Clarke, and I dare say I should have thought a page of small type, but I was cut short by a beggar who had come behind me, and was making the usual appeals. Of course I looked round, and this beggar turned out to be what was left of an old friend of mine, a man named Herbert. I asked him how he had come to such a wretched pass, and he told me. We walked up and down one of those long and dark Soho streets, and there I listened to his story. He said he had married a beautiful girl, some years younger than himself, and, as he put it, she had corrupted him body and soul. He wouldn't go into details; he said he dare not, that what he had seen and heard haunted him by night and day, and when I looked in his face I knew he was speaking the truth. There was something about the man that made me shiver. I don't know why, but it was there. I gave him a little money and sent him away, and I assure you that when he was gone I gasped for breath. His presence seemed to chill one's blood."

"Isn't this all just a little fanciful, Villiers? I suppose the poor fellow had made an imprudent marriage, and, in plain English, gone to the bad."

"Well, listen to this." Villiers told Clarke the story he had heard from Austin.

"You see," he concluded, "there can be but little doubt that this Mr. Blank, whoever he was, died of sheer terror; he saw something so awful, so terrible, that it cut short his life. And what he saw, he most certainly saw in that house, which, somehow or other, had got a bad name in the neighbourhood. I had the curiosity to go and look at the place for myself. It's a saddening kind of street; the houses are old enough to be mean and dreary, but not old enough to be quaint. As far as I could see most of them are let in lodgings, furnished and unfurnished, and almost every door has three bells to it. Here and there the ground floors have been made into shops of the commonest kind; it's a dismal street in every way. I found Number 20 was to let, and I went to the agent's and got the key. Of course I should have heard nothing of the Herberts in that quarter, but I asked the man, fair and square, how long they had left the house and whether there had been other tenants in the meanwhile. He looked at me queerly for a minute, and told me the Herberts had left immediately after the unpleasantness, as he called it, and since then the house had been empty."

Mr. Villiers paused for a moment.

"I have always been rather fond of going over empty houses; there's a sort of fascination about the desolate empty rooms, with the nails sticking in the walls, and the dust thick upon the window-sills. But I didn't enjoy going over Number 20, Paul Street. I had hardly put my foot inside the passage when I noticed a queer, heavy feeling about the air of the house. Of course all empty houses are stuffy, and so forth, but this was something quite different; I can't describe it to you, but it seemed to stop the breath. I went into the front room and the back room, and the kitchens downstairs; they were all dirty and dusty enough, as you would expect, but there was something strange about them all. I couldn't define it to you, I only know I felt queer. It was one of the rooms on the first floor, though, that was the worst. It was a largish room, and once on a time the paper must have been cheerful enough, but when I saw it, paint, paper, and everything were most doleful. But the room was full of horror; I felt my teeth grinding as I put my hand on the door, and when I went in, I thought I should have fallen fainting to the floor. However, I pulled myself together, and stood against the end wall, wondering what on earth there could be about the room to make my limbs tremble, and my heart beat as if I were at the hour of death. In one corner there was a pile of newspapers littered on the floor, and I began looking at them; they were papers of three or four years ago, some of them half torn, and some crumpled as if they had been used for packing. I turned the whole pile over, and amongst them I found a curious drawing; I will show it to you presently. But I couldn't stay in the room; I felt it was overpowering me. I was thankful to come out, safe and sound, into the open air. People stared at me as I walked along the street, and one man said I was drunk. I was staggering about from one side of the pavement to the other, and it was as much as I could do to take the key back to the agent and get home. I was in bed for a week, suffering from what my doctor called nervous shock and exhaustion. One of those days I was reading the evening paper, and happened to notice a paragraph headed: 'Starved to Death.' It was the usual style of thing; a model lodging-house in Marylebone, a door locked for several days, and a dead man in his chair when they broke in. 'The deceased,' said the paragraph, 'was known as Charles Herbert, and is believed to have been once a prosperous country gentleman. His name was familiar to the public three years ago in connection with the mysterious death in Paul Street, Tottenham Court Road, the deceased being the tenant of the house Number 20, in the area of which a gentleman of good position was found dead under circumstances not devoid of suspicion.' A tragic ending, wasn't it? But after all, if what he told me were true, which I am sure it was, the man's life was all a tragedy, and a tragedy of a stranger sort than they put on the boards."

"And that is the story, is it?" said Clarke musingly.

"Yes, that is the story."

"Well, really, Villiers, I scarcely know what to say about it. There are, no doubt, circumstances in the case which seem peculiar, the finding of the dead man in the area of Herbert's house, for instance, and the extraordinary opinion of the physician as to the cause of death; but, after all, it is conceivable that the facts may be explained in a straightforward manner. As to your own sensations, when you went to see the house, I would suggest that they were due to a vivid imagination; you must have been brooding, in a semi-conscious way, over what you had heard. I don't exactly see what more can be said or done in the matter; you evidently think there is a mystery of some kind, but Herbert is dead; where then do you propose to look?"

"I propose to look for the woman; the woman whom he married. She is the mystery."

The two men sat silent by the fireside; Clarke secretly congratulating himself on having successfully kept up the character of advocate of the commonplace, and Villiers wrapped in his gloomy fancies.

"I think I will have a cigarette," he said at last, and put his hand in his pocket to feel for the cigarette-case.

"Ah!" he said, starting slightly, "I forgot I had something to show you. You remember my saying that I had found a rather curious sketch amongst the pile of old newspapers at the house in Paul Street? Here it is."

Villiers drew out a small thin parcel from his pocket. It was covered with brown paper, and secured with string, and the knots were troublesome. In spite of himself Clarke felt inquisitive; he bent forward on his chair as Villiers painfully undid the string, and unfolded the outer covering. Inside was a second wrapping of tissue, and Villiers took it off and handed the small piece of paper to Clarke without a word.

There was dead silence in the room for five minutes or more; the two man sat so still that they could hear the ticking of the tall old-fashioned clock that stood outside in the hall, and in the mind of one of them the slow monotony of sound woke up a far, far memory. He was looking intently at the small pen-and-ink sketch of the woman's head; it had evidently been drawn with great care, and by a true artist, for the woman's soul looked out of the eyes, and the lips were parted with a strange smile. Clarke gazed still at the face; it brought to his memory one summer evening, long ago; he saw again the long lovely valley, the river winding between the hills, the meadows and the cornfields, the dull red sun, and the cold white mist rising from the water. He heard a voice speaking to him across the waves of many years, and saying "Clarke, Mary will see the god Pan!" and then he was standing in the grim room beside the doctor, listening to the heavy ticking of the clock, waiting and watching, watching the figure lying on the green char beneath the lamplight. Mary rose up, and he looked into her eyes, and his heart grew cold within him.

"Who is this woman?" he said at last. His voice was dry and hoarse.

"That is the woman who Herbert married."

Clarke looked again at the sketch; it was not Mary after all. There certainly was Mary's face, but there was something else, something he had not seen on Mary's features when the white-clad girl entered the laboratory with the doctor, nor at her terrible awakening, nor when she lay grinning on the bed.  Whatever it was, the glance that came from those eyes, the smile on the full lips, or the expression of the whole face, Clarke shuddered before it at his inmost soul, and thought, unconsciously, of Dr. Phillip's words, "the most vivid presentment of evil I have ever seen."  He turned the paper over mechanically in his hand and glanced at the back.

"Good God!  Clarke, what is the matter?  You are as white as death."

Villiers had started wildly from his chair, as Clarke fell back with a groan, and let the paper drop from his hands.

"I don't feel very well, Villiers, I am subject to these attacks.  Pour me out a little wine; thanks, that will do.  I shall feel better in a few minutes."

Villiers picked up the fallen sketch and turned it over as Clarke had done.

"You saw that?" he said.  "That's how I identified it as being a portrait of Herbert's wife, or I should say his widow.  How do you feel now?"

"Better, thanks, it was only a passing faintness.  I don't think I quite catch your meaning.  What did you say enabled you to identify the picture?"

"This word—'Helen'—was written on the back. Didn't I tell you her name was Helen?  Yes; Helen Vaughan."

Clarke groaned; there could be no shadow of doubt.

"Now, don't you agree with me," said Villiers, "that in the story I have told you to-night, and in the part this woman plays in it, there are some very strange points?"

"Yes, Villiers," Clarke muttered, "it is a strange story indeed; a strange story indeed.  You must give me time to think it over; I may be able to help you or I may not. Must you be going now? Well, good-night, Villiers, good-night. Come and see me in the course of a week."

## The Letter Of Advice

"Do you know, Austin," said Villiers, as the two friends were pacing sedately along Piccadilly one pleasant morning in May, "do you know I am convinced that what you told me about Paul Street and the Herberts is a mere episode in an extraordinary history? I may as well confess to you that when I asked you about Herbert a few months ago I had just seen him."

"You had seen him? Where?"

"He begged of me in the street one night. He was in the most pitiable plight, but I recognized the man, and I got him to tell me his history, or at least the outline of it. In brief, it amounted to this—he had been ruined by his wife."

"In what manner?"

"He would not tell me; he would only say that she had destroyed him, body and soul. The man is dead now."

"And what has become of his wife?"

"Ah, that's what I should like to know, and I mean to find her sooner or later. I know a man named Clarke, a dry fellow, in fact a man of business, but shrewd enough. You understand my meaning; not shrewd in the mere business sense of the word, but a man who really knows something about men and life. Well, I laid the case before him, and he was evidently impressed. He said it needed consideration, and asked me to come again in the course of a week. A few days later I received this extraordinary letter."

Austin took the envelope, drew out the letter, and read it curiously. It ran as follows:—

"MY DEAR VILLIERS,—I have thought over the matter on which you consulted me the other night, and my advice to you is this. Throw the portrait into the fire, blot out the story from your mind. Never give it another thought, Villiers, or you will be sorry. You will think, no doubt, that I am in possession of some secret information, and to a certain extent that is the case. But I only know a little; I am like a traveller who has peered over an abyss, and has drawn back in terror. What I know is strange enough and horrible enough, but beyond my knowledge there are depths and horrors more frightful still, more incredible than any tale told of winter nights about the fire. I have resolved, and nothing shall shake that resolve, to explore no whit farther, and if you value your happiness you will make the same determination.

"Come and see me by all means; but we will talk on more cheerful topics than this."

Austin folded the letter methodically, and returned it to Villiers.

"It is certainly an extraordinary letter," he said, "what does he mean by the portrait?"

"Ah! I forgot to tell you I have been to Paul Street and have made a discovery."

Villiers told his story as he had told it to Clarke, and Austin listened in silence. He seemed puzzled.

"How very curious that you should experience such an unpleasant sensation in that room!" he said at length. "I hardly gather that it was a mere matter of the imagination; a feeling of repulsion, in short."

"No, it was more physical than mental. It was as if I were inhaling at every breath some deadly fume, which seemed to penetrate to every nerve and bone and sinew of my body. I felt racked from head to foot, my eyes began to grow dim; it was like the entrance of death."

"Yes, yes, very strange certainly. You see, your friend confesses that there is some very black story connected with this woman. Did you notice any particular emotion in him when you were telling your tale?"

"Yes, I did. He became very faint, but he assured me that it was a mere passing attack to which he was subject."

"Did you believe him?"

"I did at the time, but I don't now. He heard what I had to say with a good deal of indifference, till I showed him the portrait. It was then that he was seized with the attack of which I spoke. He looked ghastly, I assure you."

"Then he must have seen the woman before. But there might be another explanation; it might have been the name, and not the face, which was familiar to him. What do you think?"

"I couldn't say. To the best of my belief it was after turning the portrait in his hands that he nearly dropped from the chair. The name, you know, was written on the back."

"Quite so. After all, it is impossible to come to any resolution in a case like this. I hate melodrama, and nothing strikes me as more commonplace and tedious than the ordinary ghost story of commerce; but really, Villiers, it looks as if there were something very queer at the bottom of all this."

The two men had, without noticing it, turned up Ashley Street, leading northward from Piccadilly. It was a long street, and rather a gloomy one, but here and there a brighter taste had illuminated the dark houses with flowers, and gay curtains, and a cheerful paint on the doors. Villiers glanced up as Austin stopped speaking, and looked at one of these houses; geraniums, red and white, drooped from every sill, and daffodil-coloured curtains were draped back from each window.

"It looks cheerful, doesn't it?" he said.

"Yes, and the inside is still more cheery. One of the pleasantest houses of the season, so I have heard. I haven't been there myself, but I've met several men who have, and they tell me it's uncommonly jovial."

"Whose house is it?"

"A Mrs. Beaumont's."

"And who is she?"

"I couldn't tell you. I have heard she comes from South America, but after all, who she is is of little consequence. She is a very wealthy woman, there's no doubt of that, and some of the best people have taken her up. I hear she has some wonderful claret, really marvellous wine, which must have cost a fabulous sum. Lord Argentine was telling me about it; he was there last Sunday evening. He assures me he has never tasted such a wine, and Argentine, as you know, is an expert. By the way, that reminds me, she must be an oddish sort of woman, this Mrs. Beaumont. Argentine asked her how old the wine was, and what do you think she said? 'About a thousand years, I believe.' Lord Argentine thought she was chaffing him, you know, but when he laughed she said she was speaking quite seriously and offered to show him the jar. Of course, he couldn't say anything more after that; but it seems rather antiquated for a beverage, doesn't it? Why, here we are at my rooms. Come in, won't you?"

"Thanks, I think I will. I haven't seen the curiosity-shop for a while."

It was a room furnished richly, yet oddly, where every jar and bookcase and table, and every rug and jar and ornament seemed to be a thing apart, preserving each its own individuality.

"Anything fresh lately?" said Villiers after a while.

"No; I think not; you saw those queer jugs, didn't you? I thought so. I don't think I have come across anything for the last few weeks."

Austin glanced around the room from cupboard to cupboard, from shelf to shelf, in search of some new oddity. His eyes fell at last on an odd chest, pleasantly and quaintly carved, which stood in a dark corner of the room.

"Ah," he said, "I was forgetting, I have got something to show you." Austin unlocked the chest, drew out a thick quarto volume, laid it on the table, and resumed the cigar he had put down.

"Did you know Arthur Meyrick the painter, Villiers?"

"A little; I met him two or three times at the house of a friend of mine. What has become of him? I haven't heard his name mentioned for some time."

"He's dead."

"You don't say so! Quite young, wasn't he?"

"Yes; only thirty when he died."

"What did he die of?"

"I don't know. He was an intimate friend of mine, and a thoroughly good fellow. He used to come here and talk to me for hours, and he was one of the best talkers I have met. He could even talk about painting, and that's more than can be said of most painters. About eighteen months ago he was feeling rather overworked, and partly at my suggestion he went off on a sort of roving expedition, with no very definite end or aim about it. I believe New York was to be his first port, but I never heard from him. Three months ago I got this book, with a very civil letter from an English doctor practising at Buenos Ayres, stating that he had attended the late Mr. Meyrick during his illness, and that the deceased had expressed an earnest wish that the enclosed packet should be sent to me after his death. That was all."

"And haven't you written for further particulars?"

"I have been thinking of doing so. You would advise me to write to the doctor?"

"Certainly. And what about the book?"

"It was sealed up when I got it. I don't think the doctor had seen it."

"It is something very rare? Meyrick was a collector, perhaps?"

"No, I think not, hardly a collector. Now, what do you think of these Ainu jugs?"

"They are peculiar, but I like them. But aren't you going to show me poor Meyrick's legacy?"

"Yes, yes, to be sure. The fact is, it's rather a peculiar sort of thing, and I haven't shown it to any one. I wouldn't say anything about it if I were you. There it is."

Villiers took the book, and opened it at haphazard.

"It isn't a printed volume, then?" he said.

"No. It is a collection of drawings in black and white by my poor friend Meyrick."

Villiers turned to the first page, it was blank; the second bore a brief inscription, which he read:

*Silet per diem universus, nec sine horrore secretus est; lucet nocturnis ignibus, chorus Aegipanum undique personatur: audiuntur et cantus tibiarum, et tinnitus cymbalorum per oram maritimam.*

On the third page was a design which made Villiers start and look up at Austin; he was gazing abstractedly out of the window. Villiers turned page after page, absorbed, in spite of himself, in the frightful Walpurgis Night of evil, strange monstrous evil, that the dead artist had set forth in hard black and white. The figures of Fauns and Satyrs and Aegipans danced before his eyes, the darkness of the thicket, the dance on the mountain-top, the scenes by lonely shores, in green vineyards, by rocks and desert places, passed before him: a world before which the human soul seemed to shrink back and shudder. Villiers whirled over the remaining pages; he had seen enough, but the picture on the last leaf caught his eye, as he almost closed the book.

"Austin!"

"Well, what is it?"

"Do you know who that is?"

It was a woman's face, alone on the white page.

"Know who it is? No, of course not."

"I do."

"Who is it?"

"It is Mrs. Herbert."

"Are you sure?"

"I am perfectly sure of it. Poor Meyrick! He is one more chapter in her history."

"But what do you think of the designs?"

"They are frightful. Lock the book up again, Austin. If I were you I would burn it; it must be a terrible companion even though it be in a chest."

"Yes, they are singular drawings. But I wonder what connection there could be between Meyrick and Mrs. Herbert, or what link between her and these designs?"

"Ah, who can say? It is possible that the matter may end here, and we shall never know, but in my own opinion this Helen Vaughan, or Mrs. Herbert, is only the beginning. She will come back to London, Austin; depend on it, she will come back, and we shall hear more about her then. I doubt it will be very pleasant news."

## The Suicides

Lord Argentine was a great favourite in London Society. At twenty he had been a poor man, decked with the surname of an illustrious family, but forced to earn a livelihood as best he could, and the most speculative of money-lenders would not have entrusted him with fifty pounds on the chance of his ever changing his name for a title, and his poverty for a great fortune. His father had been near enough to the fountain of good things to secure one of the family livings, but the son, even if he had taken orders, would scarcely have obtained so much as this, and moreover felt no vocation for the ecclesiastical estate. Thus he fronted the world with no better armour than the bachelor's gown and the wits of a younger son's grandson, with which equipment he contrived in some way to make a very tolerable fight of it. At twenty-five Mr. Charles Aubernon saw himself still a man of struggles and of warfare with the world, but out of the seven who stood before him and the high places of his family three only remained. These three, however, were "good lives," but yet not proof against the Zulu assegais and typhoid fever, and so one morning Aubernon woke up and found himself Lord Argentine, a man of thirty who had faced the difficulties of existence, and had conquered. The situation amused him immensely, and he resolved that riches should be as pleasant to him as poverty had always been. Argentine, after some little consideration, came to the conclusion that dining, regarded as a fine art, was perhaps the most amusing pursuit open to fallen humanity, and thus his dinners became famous in London, and an invitation to his table a thing covetously desired. After ten years of lordship and dinners Argentine still declined to be jaded, still persisted in enjoying life, and by a kind of infection had become recognized as the cause of joy in others, in short, as the best of company. His sudden and tragical death therefore caused a wide and deep sensation. People could scarcely believe it, even though the newspaper was before their eyes, and the cry of "Mysterious Death of a Nobleman" came ringing up from the street. But there stood the brief paragraph: "Lord Argentine was found dead this morning by his valet under distressing circumstances. It is stated that there can be no doubt that his lordship committed suicide, though no motive can be assigned for the act. The deceased nobleman was widely known in society, and much liked for his genial manner and sumptuous hospitality. He is succeeded by," etc., etc.

By slow degrees the details came to light, but the case still remained a mystery. The chief witness at the inquest was the deceased's valet, who said that the night before his death Lord Argentine had dined with a lady of good position, whose named was suppressed in the newspaper reports. At about eleven o'clock Lord Argentine had returned, and informed his man that he should not require his services till the next morning. A little later the valet had occasion to cross the hall and was somewhat astonished to see his master quietly letting himself out at the front door. He had taken off his evening clothes, and was dressed in a Norfolk coat and knickerbockers, and wore a low brown hat. The valet had no reason to suppose that Lord Argentine had seen him, and though his master rarely kept late hours, thought little of the occurrence till the next morning, when he knocked at the bedroom door at a quarter to nine as usual. He received no answer, and, after knocking two or three times, entered the room, and saw Lord Argentine's body leaning forward at an angle from the bottom of the bed. He found that his master had tied a cord securely to one of the short bed-posts, and, after making a running noose and slipping it round his neck, the unfortunate man must have resolutely fallen forward, to die by slow strangulation. He was dressed in the light suit in which the valet had seen him go out, and the doctor who was summoned pronounced that life had been extinct for more than four hours. All papers, letters, and so forth seemed in perfect order, and nothing was discovered which pointed in the most remote way to any scandal either great or small. Here the evidence ended; nothing more could be discovered. Several persons had been present at the dinner-party at which Lord Augustine had assisted, and to all these he seemed in his usual genial spirits. The valet, indeed, said he thought his master appeared a little excited when he came home, but confessed that the alteration in his manner was very slight, hardly noticeable, indeed. It seemed hopeless to seek for any clue, and the suggestion that Lord Argentine had been suddenly attacked by acute suicidal mania was generally accepted.

It was otherwise, however, when within three weeks, three more gentlemen, one of them a nobleman, and the two others men of good position and ample means, perished miserably in the almost precisely the same manner. Lord Swanleigh was found one morning in his dressing-room, hanging from a peg affixed to the wall, and Mr. Collier-Stuart and Mr. Herries had chosen to die as Lord Argentine. There was no explanation in either case; a few bald facts; a living man in the evening, and a body with a black swollen face in the morning. The police had been forced to confess themselves powerless to arrest or to explain the sordid murders of Whitechapel; but before the horrible suicides of Piccadilly and Mayfair they were dumbfounded, for not even the mere ferocity which did duty as an explanation of the crimes of the East End, could be of service in the West. Each of these men who had resolved to die a tortured shameful death was rich, prosperous, and to all appearances in love with the world, and not the acutest research should ferret out any shadow of a lurking motive in either case. There was a horror in the air, and men looked at one another's faces when they met, each wondering whether the other was to be the victim of the fifth nameless tragedy. Journalists sought in vain for their scrapbooks for materials whereof to concoct reminiscent articles; and the morning paper was unfolded in many a house with a feeling of awe; no man knew when or where the next blow would light.

A short while after the last of these terrible events, Austin came to see Mr. Villiers. He was curious to know whether Villiers had succeeded in discovering any fresh traces of Mrs. Herbert, either through Clarke or by other sources, and he asked the question soon after he had sat down.

"No," said Villiers, "I wrote to Clarke, but he remains obdurate, and I have tried other channels, but without any result. I can't find out what became of Helen Vaughan after she left Paul Street, but I think she must have gone abroad. But to tell the truth, Austin, I haven't paid much attention to the matter for the last few weeks; I knew poor Herries intimately, and his terrible death has been a great shock to me, a great shock."

"I can well believe it," answered Austin gravely, "you know Argentine was a friend of mine. If I remember rightly, we were speaking of him that day you came to my rooms."

"Yes; it was in connection with that house in Ashley Street, Mrs. Beaumont's house. You said something about Argentine's dining there."

"Quite so. Of course you know it was there Argentine dined the night before—before his death."

"No, I had not heard that."

"Oh, yes; the name was kept out of the papers to spare Mrs. Beaumont. Argentine was a great favourite of hers, and it is said she was in a terrible state for sometime after."

A curious look came over Villiers' face; he seemed undecided whether to speak or not. Austin began again.

"I never experienced such a feeling of horror as when I read the account of Argentine's death. I didn't understand it at the time, and I don't now. I knew him well, and it completely passes my understanding for what possible cause he —or any of the others for the matter of that—could have resolved in cold blood to die in such an awful manner. You know how men babble away each other's characters in London, you may be sure any buried scandal or hidden skeleton would have been brought to light in such a case as this; but nothing of the sort has taken place. As for the theory of mania, that is very well, of course, for the coroner's jury, but everybody knows that it's all nonsense. Suicidal mania is not small-pox."

Austin relapsed into gloomy silence. Villiers sat silent, also, watching his friend. The expression of indecision still fleeted across his face; he seemed as if weighing his thoughts in the balance, and the considerations he was resolving left him still silent. Austin tried to shake off the remembrance of tragedies as hopeless and perplexed as the labyrinth of Daedalus, and began to talk in an indifferent voice of the more pleasant incidents and adventures of the season.

"That Mrs. Beaumont," he said, "of whom we were speaking, is a great success; she has taken London almost by storm. I met her the other night at Fulham's; she is really a remarkable woman."

"You have met Mrs. Beaumont?"

"Yes; she had quite a court around her. She would be called very handsome, I suppose, and yet there is something about her face which I didn't like. The features are exquisite, but the expression is strange. And all the time I was looking at her, and afterwards, when I was going home, I had a curious feeling that very expression was in some way or another familiar to me."

"You must have seen her in the Row."

"No, I am sure I never set eyes on the woman before; it is that which makes it puzzling. And to the best of my belief I have never seen anyone like her; what I felt was a kind of dim far-off memory, vague but persistent. The only sensation I can compare it to, is that odd feeling one sometimes has in a dream, when fantastic cities and wondrous lands and phantom personages appear familiar and accustomed."

Villiers nodded and glanced aimlessly round the room, possibly in search of something on which to turn the conversation. His eyes fell on an old chest somewhat like that in which the artist's strange legacy lay hid beneath a Gothic scutcheon.

"Have you written to the doctor about poor Meyrick?" he asked.

"Yes; I wrote asking for full particulars as to his illness and death. I don't expect to have an answer for another three weeks or a month. I thought I might as well inquire whether Meyrick knew an Englishwoman named Herbert, and if so, whether the doctor could give me any information about her. But it's very possible that Meyrick fell in with her at New York, or Mexico, or San Francisco; I have no idea as to the extent or direction of his travels."

"Yes, and it's very possible that the woman may have more than one name."

"Exactly. I wish I had thought of asking you to lend me the portrait of her which you possess. I might have enclosed it in my letter to Dr. Matthews."

"So you might; that never occurred to me. We might send it now. Hark! what are those boys calling?"

While the two men had been talking together a confused noise of shouting had been gradually growing louder. The noise rose from the eastward and swelled down Piccadilly, drawing nearer and nearer, a very torrent of sound; surging up streets usually quiet, and making every window a frame for a face, curious or excited. The cries and voices came echoing up the silent street where Villiers lived, growing more distinct as they advanced, and, as Villiers spoke, an answer rang up from the pavement:

"The West End Horrors; Another Awful Suicide; Full Details!"

Austin rushed down the stairs and bought a paper and read out the paragraph to Villiers as the uproar in the street rose and fell. The window was open and the air seemed full of noise and terror.

"Another gentleman has fallen a victim to the terrible epidemic of suicide which for the last month has prevailed in the West End. Mr. Sidney Crashaw, of Stoke House, Fulham, and King's Pomeroy, Devon, was found, after a prolonged search, hanging dead from the branch of a tree in his garden at one o'clock today. The deceased gentleman dined last night at the Carlton Club and seemed in his usual health and spirits. He left the club at about ten o'clock, and was seen walking leisurely up St. James's Street a little later. Subsequent to this his movements cannot be traced. On the discovery of the body medical aid was at once summoned, but life had evidently been long extinct. So far as is known, Mr. Crashaw had no trouble or anxiety of any kind. This painful suicide, it will be remembered, is the fifth of the kind in the last month. The authorities at Scotland Yard are unable to suggest any explanation of these terrible occurrences."

Austin put down the paper in mute horror.

"I shall leave London to-morrow," he said, "it is a city of nightmares. How awful this is, Villiers!"

Mr. Villiers was sitting by the window quietly looking out into the street. He had listened to the newspaper report attentively, and the hint of indecision was no longer on his face.

"Wait a moment, Austin," he replied, "I have made up my mind to mention a little matter that occurred last night. It stated, I think, that Crashaw was last seen alive in St. James's Street shortly after ten?"

"Yes, I think so. I will look again. Yes, you are quite right."

"Quite so. Well, I am in a position to contradict that statement at all events. Crashaw was seen after that; considerably later indeed."

"How do you know?"

"Because I happened to see Crashaw myself at about two o'clock this morning."

"You saw Crashaw? You, Villiers?"

"Yes, I saw him quite distinctly; indeed, there were but a few feet between us."

"Where, in Heaven's name, did you see him?"

"Not far from here. I saw him in Ashley Street. He was just leaving a house."

"Did you notice what house it was?"

"Yes. It was Mrs. Beaumont's."

"Villiers! Think what you are saying; there must be some mistake. How could Crashaw be in Mrs. Beaumont's house at two o'clock in the morning? Surely, surely, you must have been dreaming, Villiers; you were always rather fanciful."

"No; I was wide awake enough. Even if I had been dreaming as you say, what I saw would have roused me effectually."

"What you saw? What did you see? Was there anything strange about Crashaw? But I can't believe it; it is impossible."

"Well, if you like I will tell you what I saw, or if you please, what I think I saw, and you can judge for yourself."

"Very good, Villiers."

The noise and clamour of the street had died away, though now and then the sound of shouting still came from the distance, and the dull, leaden silence seemed like the quiet after an earthquake or a storm. Villiers turned from the window and began speaking.

"I was at a house near Regent's Park last night, and when I came away the fancy took me to walk home instead of taking a hansom. It was a clear pleasant night enough, and after a few minutes I had the streets pretty much to myself. It's a curious thing, Austin, to be alone in London at night, the gas-lamps stretching away in perspective, and the dead silence, and then perhaps the rush and clatter of a hansom on the stones, and the fire starting up under the horse's hoofs. I walked along pretty briskly, for I was feeling a little tired of being out in the night, and as the clocks were striking two I turned down Ashley Street, which, you know, is on my way. It was quieter than ever there, and the lamps were fewer; altogether, it looked as dark and gloomy as a forest in winter. I had done about half the length of the street when I heard a door closed very softly, and naturally I looked up to see who was abroad like myself at such an hour. As it happens, there is a street lamp close to the house in question, and I saw a man standing on the step. He had just shut the door and his face was towards me, and I recognized Crashaw directly. I never knew him to speak to, but I had often seen him, and I am positive that I was not mistaken in my man. I looked into his face for a moment, and then—I will confess the truth—I set off at a good run, and kept it up till I was within my own door."

"Why?"

"Why? Because it made my blood run cold to see that man's face. I could never have supposed that such an infernal medley of passions could have glared out of any human eyes; I almost fainted as I looked. I knew I had looked into the eyes of a lost soul, Austin, the man's outward form remained, but all hell was within it. Furious lust, and hate that was like fire, and the loss of all hope and horror that seemed to shriek aloud to the night, though his teeth were shut; and the utter blackness of despair. I am sure that he did not see me; he saw nothing that you or I can see, but what he saw I hope we never shall. I do not know when he died; I suppose in an hour, or perhaps two, but when I passed down Ashley Street and heard the closing door, that man no longer belonged to this world; it was a devil's face I looked upon."

There was an interval of silence in the room when Villiers ceased speaking. The light was failing, and all the tumult of an hour ago was quite hushed. Austin had bent his head at the close of the story, and his hand covered his eyes.

"What can it mean?" he said at length.

"Who knows, Austin, who knows? It's a black business, but I think we had better keep it to ourselves, for the present at any rate. I will see if I cannot learn anything about that house through private channels of information, and if I do light upon anything I will let you know."

## The Encounter In Soho

Three weeks later Austin received a note from Villiers, asking him to call either that afternoon or the next. He chose the nearer date, and found Villiers sitting as usual by the window, apparently lost in meditation on the drowsy traffic of the street. There was a bamboo table by his side, a fantastic thing, enriched with gilding and queer painted scenes, and on it lay a little pile of papers arranged and docketed as neatly as anything in Mr. Clarke's office.

"Well, Villiers, have you made any discoveries in the last three weeks?"

"I think so; I have here one or two memoranda which struck me as singular, and there is a statement to which I shall call your attention."

"And these documents relate to Mrs. Beaumont? It was really Crashaw whom you saw that night standing on the doorstep of the house in Ashley Street?"

"As to that matter my belief remains unchanged, but neither my inquiries nor their results have any special relation to Crashaw. But my investigations have had a strange issue. I have found out who Mrs. Beaumont is!"

"Who is she? In what way do you mean?"

"I mean that you and I know her better under another name."

"What name is that?"

"Herbert."

"Herbert!" Austin repeated the word, dazed with astonishment.

"Yes, Mrs. Herbert of Paul Street, Helen Vaughan of earlier adventures unknown to me. You had reason to recognize the expression of her face; when you go home look at the face in Meyrick's book of horrors, and you will know the sources of your recollection."

"And you have proof of this?"

"Yes, the best of proof; I have seen Mrs. Beaumont, or shall we say Mrs. Herbert?"

"Where did you see her?"

"Hardly in a place where you would expect to see a lady who lives in Ashley Street, Piccadilly. I saw her entering a house in one of the meanest and most disreputable streets in Soho. In fact, I had made an appointment, though not with her, and she was precise to both time and place."

"All this seems very wonderful, but I cannot call it incredible. You must remember, Villiers, that I have seen this woman, in the ordinary adventure of London society, talking and laughing, and sipping her coffee in a commonplace drawing-room with commonplace people. But you know what you are saying."

"I do; I have not allowed myself to be led by surmises or fancies. It was with no thought of finding Helen Vaughan that I searched for Mrs. Beaumont in the dark waters of the life of London, but such has been the issue."

"You must have been in strange places, Villiers."

"Yes, I have been in very strange places. It would have been useless, you know, to go to Ashley Street, and ask Mrs. Beaumont to give me a short sketch of her previous history. No; assuming, as I had to assume, that her record was not of the cleanest, it would be pretty certain that at some previous time she must have moved in circles not quite so refined as her present ones. If you see mud at the top of a stream, you may be sure that it was once at the bottom. I went to the bottom. I have always been fond of diving into Queer Street for my amusement, and I found my knowledge of that locality and its inhabitants very useful. It is, perhaps, needless to say that my friends had never heard the name of Beaumont, and as I had never seen the lady, and was quite unable to describe her, I had to set to work in an indirect way. The people there know me; I have been able to do some of them a service now and again, so they made no difficulty about giving their information; they were aware I had no communication direct or indirect with Scotland Yard. I had to cast out a good many lines, though, before I got what I wanted, and when I landed the fish I did not for a moment suppose it was my fish. But I listened to what I was told out of a constitutional liking for useless information, and I found myself in possession of a very curious story, though, as I imagined, not the story I was looking for. It was to this effect. Some five or six years ago, a woman named Raymond suddenly made her appearance in the neighbourhood to which I am referring. She was described to me as being quite young, probably not more than seventeen or eighteen, very handsome, and looking as if she came from the country. I should be wrong in saying that she found her level in going to this particular quarter, or associating with these people, for from what I was told, I should think the worst den in London far too good for her. The person from whom I got my information, as you may suppose, no great Puritan, shuddered and grew sick in telling me of the nameless infamies which were laid to her charge. After living there for a year, or perhaps a little more, she disappeared as suddenly as she came, and they saw nothing of her till about the time of the Paul Street case. At first she came to her old haunts only occasionally, then more frequently, and finally took up her abode there as before, and remained for six or eight months. It's of no use my going into details as to the life that woman led; if you want particulars you can look at Meyrick's legacy. Those designs were not drawn from his imagination. She again disappeared, and the people of the place saw nothing of her till a few months ago. My informant told me that she had taken some rooms in a house which he pointed out, and these rooms she was in the habit of visiting two or three times a week and always at ten in the morning. I was led to expect that one of these visits would be paid on a certain day about a week ago, and I accordingly managed to be on the look-out in company with my cicerone at a quarter to ten, and the hour and the lady came with equal punctuality. My friend and I were standing under an archway, a little way back from the street, but she saw us, and gave me a glance that I shall be long in forgetting. That look was quite enough for me; I knew Miss Raymond to be Mrs. Herbert; as for Mrs. Beaumont she had quite gone out of my head. She went into the house, and I watched it till four o'clock, when she came out, and then I followed her. It was a long chase, and I had to be very careful to keep a long way in the background, and yet not lose sight of the woman. She took me down to the Strand, and then to Westminster, and then up St. James's Street, and along Piccadilly. I felt queerish when I saw her turn up Ashley Street; the thought that Mrs. Herbert was Mrs. Beaumont came into my mind, but it seemed too impossible to be true. I waited at the corner, keeping my eye on her all the time, and I took particular care to note the house at which she stopped. It was the house with the gay curtains, the home of flowers, the house out of which Crashaw came the night he hanged himself in his garden. I was just going away with my discovery, when I saw an empty carriage come round and draw up in front of the house, and I came to the conclusion that Mrs. Herbert was going out for a drive, and I was right. There, as it happened, I met a man I know, and we stood talking together a little distance from the carriage-way, to which I had my back. We had not been there for ten minutes when my friend took off his hat, and I glanced round and saw the lady I had been following all day. 'Who is that?' I said, and his answer was 'Mrs. Beaumont; lives in Ashley Street.' Of course there could be no doubt after that. I don't know whether she saw me, but I don't think she did. I went home at once, and, on consideration, I thought that I had a sufficiently good case with which to go to Clarke."

"Why to Clarke?"

"Because I am sure that Clarke is in possession of facts about this woman, facts of which I know nothing."

"Well, what then?"

Mr. Villiers leaned back in his chair and looked reflectively at Austin for a moment before he answered:

"My idea was that Clarke and I should call on Mrs. Beaumont."

"You would never go into such a house as that? No, no, Villiers, you cannot do it. Besides, consider; what result..."

"I will tell you soon. But I was going to say that my information does not end here; it has been completed in an extraordinary manner.

"Look at this neat little packet of manuscript; it is paginated, you see, and I have indulged in the civil coquetry of a ribbon of red tape. It has almost a legal air, hasn't it? Run your eye over it, Austin. It is an account of the entertainment Mrs. Beaumont provided for her choicer guests. The man who wrote this escaped with his life, but I do not think he will live many years. The doctors tell him he must have sustained some severe shock to the nerves."

Austin took the manuscript, but never read it. Opening the neat pages at haphazard his eye was caught by a word and a phrase that followed it; and, sick at heart, with white lips and a cold sweat pouring like water from his temples, he flung the paper down.

"Take it away, Villiers, never speak of this again. Are you made of stone, man? Why, the dread and horror of death itself, the thoughts of the man who stands in the keen morning air on the black platform, bound, the bell tolling in his ears, and waits for the harsh rattle of the bolt, are as nothing compared to this. I will not read it; I should never sleep again."

"Very good. I can fancy what you saw. Yes; it is horrible enough; but after all, it is an old story, an old mystery played in our day, and in dim London streets instead of amidst the vineyards and the olive gardens. We know what happened to those who chanced to meet the Great God Pan, and those who are wise know that all symbols are symbols of something, not of nothing. It was, indeed, an exquisite symbol beneath which men long ago veiled their knowledge of the most awful, most secret forces which lie at the heart of all things; forces before which the souls of men must wither and die and blacken, as their bodies blacken under the electric current. Such forces cannot be named, cannot be spoken, cannot be imagined except under a veil and a symbol, a symbol to the most of us appearing a quaint, poetic fancy, to some a foolish tale. But you and I, at all events, have known something of the terror that may dwell in the secret place of life, manifested under human flesh; that which is without form taking to itself a form. Oh, Austin, how can it be? How is it that the very sunlight does not turn to blackness before this thing, the hard earth melt and boil beneath such a burden?"

Villiers was pacing up and down the room, and the beads of sweat stood out on his forehead. Austin sat silent for a while, but Villiers saw him make a sign upon his breast.

"I say again, Villiers, you will surely never enter such a house as that? You would never pass out alive."

"Yes, Austin, I shall go out alive—I, and Clarke with me."

What do you mean? You cannot, you would not dare..."

"Wait a moment. The air was very pleasant and fresh this morning; there was a breeze blowing, even through this dull street, and I thought I would take a walk. Piccadilly stretched before me a clear, bright vista, and the sun flashed on the carriages and on the quivering leaves in the park. It was a joyous morning, and men and women looked at the sky and smiled as they went about their work or their pleasure, and the wind blew as blithely as upon the meadows and the scented gorse. But somehow or other I got out of the bustle and the gaiety, and found myself walking slowly along a quiet, dull street, where there seemed to be no sunshine and no air, and where the few foot-passengers loitered as they walked, and hung indecisively about corners and archways. I walked along, hardly knowing where I was going or what I did there, but feeling impelled, as one sometimes is, to explore still further, with a vague idea of reaching some unknown goal. Thus I forged up the street, noting the small traffic of the milk-shop, and wondering at the incongruous medley of penny pipes, black tobacco, sweets, newspapers, and comic songs which here and there jostled one another in the short compass of a single window. I think it was a cold shudder that suddenly passed through me that first told me that I had found what I wanted. I looked up from the pavement and stopped before a dusty shop, above which the lettering had faded, where the red bricks of two hundred years ago had grimed to black; where the windows had gathered to themselves the dust of winters innumerable. I saw what I required; but I think it was five minutes before I had steadied myself and could walk in and ask for it in a cool voice and with a calm face. I think there must even then have been a tremor in my words, for the old man who came out of the back parlour, and fumbled slowly amongst his goods, looked oddly at me as he tied the parcel. I paid what he asked, and stood leaning by the counter, with a strange reluctance to take up my goods and go. I asked about the business, and learnt that trade was bad and the profits cut down sadly; but then the street was not what it was before traffic had been diverted, but that was done forty years ago, 'just before my father died,' he said. I got away at last, and walked along sharply; it was a dismal street indeed, and I was glad to return to the bustle and the noise. Would you like to see my purchase?"

Austin said nothing, but nodded his head slightly; he still looked white and sick. Villiers pulled out a drawer in the bamboo table, and showed Austin a long coil of cord, hard and new; and at one end was a running noose.

"It is the best hempen cord," said Villiers, "just as it used to be made for the old trade, the man told me. Not an inch of jute from end to end."

Austin set his teeth hard, and stared at Villiers, growing whiter as he looked.

"You would not do it," he murmured at last. "You would not have blood on your hands. My God!" he exclaimed, with sudden vehemence, "you cannot mean this, Villiers, that you will make yourself a hangman?"

"No. I shall offer a choice, and leave Helen Vaughan alone with this cord in a locked room for fifteen minutes. If when we go in it is not done, I shall call the nearest policeman. That is all."

"I must go now. I cannot stay here any longer; I cannot bear this. Good-night."

"Good-night, Austin."

The door shut, but in a moment it was open again, and Austin stood, white and ghastly, in the entrance.

"I was forgetting," he said, "that I too have something to tell. I have received a letter from Dr. Harding of Buenos Ayres. He says that he attended Meyrick for three weeks before his death."

"And does he say what carried him off in the prime of life? It was not fever?"

"No, it was not fever. According to the doctor, it was an utter collapse of the whole system, probably caused by some severe shock. But he states that the patient would tell him nothing, and that he was consequently at some disadvantage in treating the case."

"Is there anything more?"

"Yes. Dr. Harding ends his letter by saying: 'I think this is all the information I can give you about your poor friend. He had not been long in Buenos Ayres, and knew scarcely any one, with the exception of a person who did not bear the best of characters, and has since left—a Mrs. Vaughan.'"

## The Fragments

*Amongst the papers of the well-known physician, Dr. Robert Matheson, of Ashley Street, Piccadilly, who died suddenly, of apoplectic seizure, at the beginning of 1892, a leaf of manuscript paper was found, covered with pencil jottings. These notes were in Latin, much abbreviated, and had evidently been made in great haste. The MS. was only deciphered with difficulty, and some words have up to the present time evaded all the efforts of the expert employed. The date, "XXV Jul. 1888," is written on the right-hand corner of the MS. The following is a translation of Dr. Matheson's manuscript.*

"Whether science would benefit by these brief notes if they could be published, I do not know, but rather doubt. But certainly I shall never take the responsibility of publishing or divulging one word of what is here written, not only on account of my oath given freely to those two persons who were present, but also because the details are too abominable. It is probably that, upon mature consideration, and after weighting the good and evil, I shall one day destroy this paper, or at least leave it under seal to my friend D., trusting in his discretion, to use it or to burn it, as he may think fit.

"As was befitting, I did all that my knowledge suggested to make sure that I was suffering under no delusion. At first astounded, I could hardly think, but in a minute's time I was sure that my pulse was steady and regular, and that I was in my real and true senses. I then fixed my eyes quietly on what was before me.

"Though horror and revolting nausea rose up within me, and an odour of corruption choked my breath, I remained firm. I was then privileged or accursed, I dare not say which, to see that which was on the bed, lying there black like ink, transformed before my eyes. The skin, and the flesh, and the muscles, and the bones, and the firm structure of the human body that I had thought to be unchangeable, and permanent as adamant, began to melt and dissolve.

"I know that the body may be separated into its elements by external agencies, but I should have refused to believe what I saw. For here there was some internal force, of which I knew nothing, that caused dissolution and change.

"Here too was all the work by which man had been made repeated before my eyes. I saw the form waver from sex to sex, dividing itself from itself, and then again reunited. Then I saw the body descend to the beasts whence it ascended, and that which was on the heights go down to the depths, even to the abyss of all being. The principle of life, which makes organism, always remained, while the outward form changed.

"The light within the room had turned to blackness, not the darkness of night, in which objects are seen dimly, for I could see clearly and without difficulty. But it was the negation of light; objects were presented to my eyes, if I may say so, without any medium, in such a manner that if there had been a prism in the room I should have seen no colours represented in it.

"I watched, and at last I saw nothing but a substance as jelly. Then the ladder was ascended again... [here the MS. is illegible] ...for one instance I saw a Form, shaped in dimness before me, which I will not farther describe. But the symbol of this form may be seen in ancient sculptures, and in paintings which survived beneath the lava, too foul to be spoken of... as a horrible and unspeakable shape, neither man nor beast, was changed into human form, there came finally death.

"I who saw all this, not without great horror and loathing of soul, here write my name, declaring all that I have set on this paper to be true.

"ROBERT MATHESON, Med. Dr."

...Such, Raymond, is the story of what I know and what I have seen. The burden of it was too heavy for me to bear alone, and yet I could tell it to none but you. Villiers, who was with me at the last, knows nothing of that awful secret of the wood, of how what we both saw die, lay upon the smooth, sweet turf amidst the summer flowers, half in sun and half in shadow, and holding the girl Rachel's hand, called and summoned those companions, and shaped in solid form, upon the earth we tread upon, the horror which we can but hint at, which we can only name under a figure. I would not tell Villiers of this, nor of that resemblance, which struck me as with a blow upon my heart, when I saw the portrait, which filled the cup of terror at the end. What this can mean I dare not guess. I know that what I saw perish was not Mary, and yet in the last agony Mary's eyes looked into mine. Whether there can be any one who can show the last link in this chain of awful mystery, I do not know, but if there be any one who can do this, you, Raymond, are the man. And if you know the secret, it rests with you to tell it or not, as you please.

I am writing this letter to you immediately on my getting back to town. I have been in the country for the last few days; perhaps you may be able to guess in which part. While the horror and wonder of London was at its height—for "Mrs. Beaumont," as I have told you, was well known in society—I wrote to my friend Dr. Phillips, giving some brief outline, or rather hint, of what happened, and asking him to tell me the name of the village where the events he had related to me occurred. He gave me the name, as he said with the less hesitation, because Rachel's father and mother were dead, and the rest of the family had gone to a relative in the State of Washington six months before. The parents, he said, had undoubtedly died of grief and horror caused by the terrible death of their daughter, and by what had gone before that death. On the evening of the day which I received Phillips' letter I was at Caermaen, and standing beneath the mouldering Roman walls, white with the winters of seventeen hundred years, I looked over the meadow where once had stood the older temple of the "God of the Deeps," and saw a house gleaming in the sunlight. It was the house where Helen had lived. I stayed at Caermaen for several days. The people of the place, I found, knew little and had guessed less. Those whom I spoke to on the matter seemed surprised that an antiquarian (as I professed myself to be) should trouble about a village tragedy, of which they gave a very commonplace version, and, as you may imagine, I told nothing of what I knew. Most of my time was spent in the great wood that rises just above the village and climbs the hillside, and goes down to the river in the valley; such another long lovely valley, Raymond, as that on which we looked one summer night, walking to and fro before your house. For many an hour I strayed through the maze of the forest, turning now to right and now to left, pacing slowly down long alleys of undergrowth, shadowy and chill, even under the midday sun, and halting beneath great oaks; lying on the short turf of a clearing where the faint sweet scent of wild roses came to me on the wind and mixed with the heavy perfume of the elder, whose mingled odour is like the odour of the room of the dead, a vapour of incense and corruption. I stood at the edges of the wood, gazing at all the pomp and procession of the foxgloves towering amidst the bracken and shining red in the broad sunshine, and beyond them into deep thickets of close undergrowth where springs boil up from the rock and nourish the water-weeds, dank and evil. But in all my wanderings I avoided one part of the wood; it was not till yesterday that I climbed to the summit of the hill, and stood upon the ancient Roman road that threads the highest ridge of the wood. Here they had walked, Helen and Rachel, along this quiet causeway, upon the pavement of green turf, shut in on either side by high banks of red earth, and tall hedges of shining beech, and here I followed in their steps, looking out, now and again, through partings in the boughs, and seeing on one side the sweep of the wood stretching far to right and left, and sinking into the broad level, and beyond, the yellow sea, and the land over the sea. On the other side was the valley and the river and hill following hill as wave on wave, and wood and meadow, and cornfield, and white houses gleaming, and a great wall of mountain, and far blue peaks in the north. And so at least I came to the place. The track went up a gentle slope, and widened out into an open space with a wall of thick undergrowth around it, and then, narrowing again, passed on into the distance and the faint blue mist of summer heat. And into this pleasant summer glade Rachel passed a girl, and left it, who shall say what? I did not stay long there.

In a small town near Caermaen there is a museum, containing for the most part Roman remains which have been found in the neighbourhood at various times. On the day after my arrival in Caermaen I walked over to the town in question, and took the opportunity of inspecting the museum. After I had seen most of the sculptured stones, the coffins, rings, coins, and fragments of tessellated pavement which the place contains, I was shown a small square pillar of white stone, which had been recently discovered in the wood of which I have been speaking, and, as I found on inquiry, in that open space where the Roman road broadens out. On one side of the pillar was an inscription, of which I took a note. Some of the letters have been defaced, but I do not think there can be any doubt as to those which I supply. The inscription is as follows:

DEVOMNODENTi
FLAvIVSSENILISPOSSvit
PROPTERNVPtias
QuaSVIDITSVBVMra

"To the great god Nodens (the god of the Great Deep or Abyss) Flavius Senilis has erected this pillar on account of the marriage which he saw beneath the shade."

The custodian of the museum informed me that local antiquaries were much puzzled, not by the inscription, or by any difficulty in translating it, but as to the circumstance or rite to which allusion is made.

...And now, my dear Clarke, as to what you tell me about Helen Vaughan, whom you say you saw die under circumstances of the utmost and almost incredible horror. I was interested in your account, but a good deal, nay all, of what you told me I knew already. I can understand the strange likeness you remarked in both the portrait and in the actual face; you have seen Helen's mother. You remember that still summer night so many years ago, when I talked to you of the world beyond the shadows, and of the god Pan. You remember Mary. She was the mother of Helen Vaughan, who was born nine months after that night.

Mary never recovered her reason. She lay, as you saw her, all the while upon her bed, and a few days after the child was born she died. I fancy that just at the last she knew me; I was standing by the bed, and the old look came into her eyes for a second, and then she shuddered and groaned and died. It was an ill work I did that night when you were present; I broke open the door of the house of life, without knowing or caring what might pass forth or enter in. I recollect your telling me at the time, sharply enough, and rightly too, in one sense, that I had ruined the reason of a human being by a foolish experiment, based on an absurd theory. You did well to blame me, but my theory was not all absurdity. What I said Mary would see she saw, but I forgot that no human eyes can look on such a sight with impunity. And I forgot, as I have just said, that when the house of life is thus thrown open, there may enter in that for which we have no name, and human flesh may become the veil of a horror one dare not express. I played with energies which I did not understand, you have seen the ending of it. Helen Vaughan did well to bind the cord about her neck and die, though the death was horrible. The blackened face, the hideous form upon the bed, changing and melting before your eyes from woman to man, from man to beast, and from beast to worse than beast, all the strange horror that you witness, surprises me but little. What you say the doctor whom you sent for saw and shuddered at I noticed long ago; I knew what I had done the moment the child was born, and when it was scarcely five years old I surprised it, not once or twice but several times with a playmate, you may guess of what kind. It was for me a constant, an incarnate horror, and after a few years I felt I could bear it no more, and I sent Helen Vaughan away. You know now what frightened the boy in the wood. The rest of the strange story, and all else that you tell me, as discovered by your friend, I have contrived to learn from time to time, almost to the last chapter. And now Helen is with her companions...

# Yeats the Magician

*Mogg Morgan*

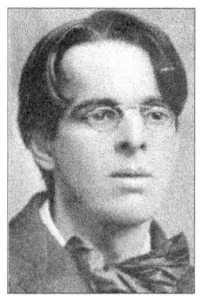

In 1995 I went on holiday to Ireland. On a day too wet to explore the limestone pavements of the Burren I made my way over to Gort, looking for the lair of the poet WB Yeats and his lifelong friend and patron LadyGregory. In an act of municipal vandalism, the remains of Coole Park, the Gregory countryseat, were pulled down in the 1960s. I suspect that following the 1921 partition of Ireland, it suffered the fate of many an Anglo Irish household and was burnt out. So the place that inspired so many magical poems is no more, although it is still possible to wander in the park, now open to the public and meditate upon those magical swans:

> Unwearied still, lover by lover,
> They paddle in the cold
> Companionable streams or climb the air;
> Their hearts have not grown old;
> Passion or conquest, wander where they will,
> Attend upon them still.

(from The Wild Swans At Coole 1919)

When in Ireland, Yeats wanted to live close to his friend Lady Gregory and he bought a ruined Norman tower house called Ballylee Castle or Thoor Ballylee and began renovation. Ireland is dotted with these gloomy monuments, built by the invading Normans to protect their new conquest from the remains of the Celtic aristocracy. The Norman invasion of Ireland really does represent the end of the Celtic world and the substitution of a more patrician Christian church for the plebeian Celtic variety. The Tower house is now one of several museums dedicated to the life and poetry of Yeats - perhaps Ireland's greatest twentieth century poet. Yeats was never able to completely fulfill his plan to make this tower his permanent base. His growing involvement in Irish politics and then ill heath necessitated another warmer home. Even so magical events occurred here, and the curators of the museum have captured this in the museum's design.

The Yeats bought the tower in 1915 but it was pretty much uninhabitable until 1918. After a magical journey through Galway and the west of Ireland, the Yeats made a point of finishing off their odyssey with a session at the tower on the equinox, i.e. c 21 September 1918. This was to be the first of many magical rituals performed in the tower, either in its rooms or occasionally, so it is said, on the roof. The roof is a particularly good place for elemental rituals; high above the surrounding trees and open to the bleak Atlantic gales, that thrust their way across the plain. Their first session had to be brief because, as they wrote in their magical diary, the place was still 'very cold'.

It is interesting to see how much Aleister Crowley followed Yeats' activities, making a point of including the Tower house as a setting for an important incident in his novel *Moonchild*, written in 1917, i.e. two years after Yeats' purchase of the place. A character in Crowley's novel called 'Gates' is magically attacked at the tower and falls to his death. The story's narrator tells us that Gates, "had been to the church in the village near Posilippo, whose tower overlooked the 'butterflynet'; and he had persuaded the priest to allow him continual access to that tower, on the pretext of being an artist. And indeed he had a *pretty amateur talent for painting in water-colours*." (p. 161 Weiser Edition, my emphasis). The 'butterfly net', is a code name used by the characters in the novel for the magical operation of creating a moonchild. That is a complex operation of sexual magick in which the participants conceive a child and then attempt to persuade a spirit of a higher spiritual entity to reincarnate into the developing foetus. Occult theory specified that the most appropriate time for such an operation be during the third month of foetal development when consciousness was said to begin in the womb. As we shall see, magical work such as this was not unknown in the Hermetic Order of the Golden Dawn, the source of Crowley's early training in magick. Crowley had never physically visited the tower and made the incorrect assumption that the tower was a disused ecclesiastical building. Thus in *Moonchild*, a magical link is established between the XVI tarot trump, the blasted tower or church and Gates' hideaway bringing about its destruction by lightning.

There was obviously no love lost between Yeats and Crowley. In his publication *The Equinox*, Crowley, in a series of articles entitled 'My Crapulous Contemporaries', lampooned many of the occultists of his day, including W B Yeats. He crudely satirized Yeats' Celtic prose drama *The Shadowy Waters*, as the 'Shadowy Dill Waters', writing that 'It is true that a sort of dreary music runs monotonously through your verses, only jarred by the occasional discords. It is as if an eternal funeral passed along, and the motor-hearse had something wrong with the ignition and the exhaust.' (*Equinox* Vol II)

You might doubt Crowley's assessment of Yeats as an artist (and magician). But bear in mind that *The Shadowy Waters* was written in 1906, years before Yeats' great revelation. Indeed, Richard Ellmann, a modern scholar with a cooler head than Crowley's, seems to share some of his assessment - Ellmann says that 'had Yeats died instead of marrying in 1917, he would have been remembered as a remarkable minor poet who achieved a diction more powerful than that of his contemporaries but who, except in a handful of poems, did not have much to say with it.'[1]

The novel *Moonchild*, like a great deal of Crowley's writing, is strangely prophetic - especially in this instance of what was *about* to happen to Yeats in the *very* year of its publication. Yeats was indeed struck by a lightning bolt out of the blue. Those with literary ambitions take note, Yeats was born in 1865 and so was fifty-two at the time, and the moral – it is never too late to start. It is also interesting in terms of magical development. Many of us learn magick over a much shorter time span that our predecessors of a few generations ago. Magical training and written material are now much more widely available. Even so, many of the more profound elements of the magical work require time and intellectual maturity if they are to really work. Yeats had been in the Hermetic Order of the Golden Dawn for the best part of twenty-eight years, by the time his real revelation and magical breakthrough came his way. He had done much important work in that organisation and before that in the Theosophical Society and diverse spiritualist groups. He waited a long time for the veil on the adytum to be lifted.

It is often assumed that Yeats' muse was Maud Gonne, the Irish nationalist and fellow member of Hermetic Order of the Golden Dawn. It is sometimes said that with her Yeats enjoyed what amounted to a spiritual marriage. This relationship became less important to him after his mundane marriage in 1917.

Relationships like Yeats and Maud Gonne can be likened to a variety of 'tantrism' called *sahajiyana* or the 'natural way'. Sahajiyans are often poets and artists who enter into secret and elicit trysts that fall outside of normal family or clan loyalties. These are what amount to largely unconsummated, unearthed love affairs. This has a very magical effect on the body, which remains, in a highly aroused state, often for many weeks, even years. By aroused, I do not necessarily mean the sexual centres, these may well be involved, but often the arousal is more noticeable in other parts of the 'psychological' anatomy. I still find the Tantrik chakra system the most convenient way to describe this - the arousal may be more noticeable in the stomach (manipura chakra), or 'heart' (anahata chakra), where it may be transferred to the throat or head chakras. This energy can be very tangible and it may be possible for it to physically flow between the corresponding chakras of the sahajiyan partners when they are in receptive mood. (See my book *Sexual Magick*, for some more information on this system.)

As there is often no satisfactory physical resolution of the passion, large amounts of psychic energy erupt into other areas, often as highly creative outbursts of poetry or art. Eventually the relationship burns itself out or the partners step over the line and the relationship falls apart. On the negative side, it seems that the pent up energy engendered by this magical practice can sometimes manifest as physical illness. Ancient medico-tantrik sources known as Ayurveda (the science of longevity), of which I am a student, say that Tuberculosis is the disease most often linked with the above psychic state and interestingly this disease is known across several cultures as a disease of lovers.

Yeats obviously felt a need to earth his highly creative magical partnership with Maud Gonne in the form of a full physical relationship, but this was not to be. Throughout their relationship Maud Gonne refused his every proposal of marriage dealing a final blow to Yeats's hopes when in 1903 she wrote to him from Paris that she had just married Major John McBride of the Irish Transvaal Brigade in the Boar War.

McBride was, according to Ellmann, not a poet, not an occultist, not a learned man and not even a good lover. It seemed a perverse choice of a husband. Predictably the effect on Yeats was devastating - it almost killed him. A London pathologist, and fellow member of the Hermetic Order of the Golden Dawn (Westcott,?) thought that he must have had tuberculosis. This was apparently confirmed by later X-ray, although luckily for Yeats the disease disappeared again. Serious as the disease was, and indeed still is, Yeats' experience of it shows that it is possible to escape its clutches. His recovery is not unusual given the help of friends and indeed the power of magick in its broadest sense.

Maud Gonne's husband John McBride was killed in the abortive Easter 1916 rising against the British colonial rule of Ireland. This event was in itself something of a magical act. The participants knew beforehand that the action was doomed to failure, but went ahead because of the effect they thought it might (and in fact did) have on the popular imagination. So McBride turned out to be a magician after all and Yeats, although he hated McBride, saw that he had 'found [his] heroic opposite'2 and Yeats, magnanimous to the last, immortalized him in the poem *Easter 1916*:

> 'This other man I had dreamed
> A drunken, vainglorious lout,
> He had done most bitter wrong
> To some who are near my heart,
> Yet I number him in the song;
> He, too, has resigned his part
> In the casual comedy;
> He, too, has been changed in his turn,
> Transformed utterly:
> A terrible beauty is born.

## The Hermetic roller coaster

Yeats' life began to pick up pace, and he entered a period that may be familiar to some modern occultists as the 'hermetic roller coaster'. Yeats rushed to Paris to again propose marriage to Maud Gonne on condition that she gave up politics. She refused. Despite this knock back, he stayed in Paris and struck up a friendship with Maud Gonne's daughter Iseult.

Iseult was Maud Gonne's daughter by a much earlier marriage. Iseult was born in 1894 in rather strange circumstances. When Yeats first met her mother Maud Gonne, she was, unbeknownst to him, already in love with a French newspaper editor by whom she had conceived a child. Sadly this child died. Yeats and his friend George Russell, who under the pseudonym AE authored a mystical book entitled *The Candle of Vision*, was comforting Maud following this untimely death. She asked them what would happen to such a tiny soul. I think it was George Russell who pronounced that 'such souls were often reborn in the same family'.

Consumed by grief, Maud Gonne found the father and took him down to the burial vault in Sacré Coeur and made love to him over the dead child's coffin! Maud Gonne conceived and the child was called Iseult. The whole story is very reminiscent of Crowley's later novel *Moonchild*. It also has important parallels with the Hindu tantrik practice of savasadhana, or meditation on a corpse. Such rites are said to be still practiced in India, although they are very secret. An experienced tantrik magician and his assistant go to the cremation ground where fresh corpses are stored awaiting cremation the next day. Whilst the assistant keeps watch, the tantrik adept prepares a terrifying ritual in which a primordial goddess is invoked into the revivified corpse. The adept take a strong psychoactive potion and the rite can result in the most terrifying visions.

Maud Gonne's daughter Iseult, was in her early twenties at the time she was befriended by the much older Yeats. Inevitably he proposed to her, and after several months of presumable hard soul searching, she too turned him down.

Shortly after this final knock back, Yeats returned to England and took up with a woman friend called Georgie Hyde Lees, a woman he had known from his days in the Hermetic Order of the Golden Dawn. In October 1917, after a whirlwind romance, he married her. Now all the fun begins. As the proverb goes, 'marry in haste, repent at leisure,' and indeed Yeats did repent. For within a few days of their marriage he was having serious doubts about the wisdom of it all and sank into one of his deepest depressions. What a mistake he thought he had made.

## Passive and active mediumship

The newlyweds were honeymooning in the Ashdown Forest in Sussex. Mrs Yeats, or 'George' as she was habitually called, seeing what a mood her husband was in thought she would do something to distract him. She was interested in psychic research and back in 1911 had helped Yeats to check the authenticity of information given him by mediums, so she knew a thing or two about parlour-room séances. As Ellmann puts it, 'she encouraged a pencil to write a sentence' 3 Here is what she wrote 'What you have done is right for both the cat and the hare.' She was the cat and the hare was Maud Gonne. The more cynically minded read into this, that George was desperate to keep her unhappy husband and used a spiritualist trick to capture his attention and eventually his love. Whatever the truth, from these small, contrived beginnings, sprang what has been described as 'the most remarkable body of materials of its kind in the history of psychical research'.

Over the course of the next three years, the couple recorded 3600 pages of automatic writing made during 450 sittings - by any standards a sizeable body of work. I wonder how many modern magicians can remember the last thirty rituals they were in, let along 400!

And those 3600 pages of research are only that part of the communication that they choose to preserve. Much of it was lost, including the record of those first few crucial days. Even so it makes Crowley/Aiwaz's *Book of the Law* look like a *billet doux*. Some of the communication was worked over by Yeats and published as a book entitled *A Vision*, which is as near as he ever got to constructing his own magical system.

The Yeats' training in the Golden Dawn would have instilled in them hostility toward common spiritualism. The Golden Dawn taught that passive mediumship was to be avoided at all costs. Passive mediumship is the kind of mediumship one can still see practiced in spiritualist churches. The medium enters a light trance and invites any spirits present to make use of him or her. The Golden Dawn taught that the medium should take a more active role, selecting and invoking appropriate spirits, which are then able to give a higher level of communication. This is not to deny remarkable results sometimes achieved by passive mediumship.[5] However, many of the examples I and other investigators have witnessed, have been far from impressive and often faked.

In the Yeats' experiments, they trod a middle path between passive and active mediumship. They often discarded large chunks of the script after later examination and checking. In fact it seems that William Yeats, was on the lookout for dodgy communications and later asked his wife for a list of the books in her library. He read every one of these books to see, if any of the more complex ideas might be derived from them - a suspicion that turned out to be quite unfounded.

## What was the purpose of the communication?

Yeats was, to use a modern idiom, 'knocked out' by the content of the 'almost illegible script'. He found it so exciting and profound that he 'offered to spend the rest of his life explaining and piecing together those scattered fragments.'

> *'No' said the communicators firmly, 'we have come to give you* metaphors *for poetry'*

And indeed, this is what happened.

William Yeats thereafter came 'to be ranked as the dominant poet of our time...largely responsible for founding a literary movement and for bringing a national theatre into being; he drew into creative energy Synge and Lady Gregory, strongly influenced a number of other writers and evolved a new way of writing verse.'6 So very different to what Crowley called a *pretty amateur talent*. The communicators were true to their words and much more besides. It is also worth bearing in mind that poetry was in times past and certainly up until the time of Yeats, seen as a magical art form. In the Celtic world, it is well known that the Bards were expected to be proficient in poetry as a sign of their adeptship. So perhaps it was for William Yeats after he received the initiation of the bridal chamber and what he called the *Gift of Harun Al Rashid*.

## The method

We can learn a lot from this. The communicators insisted that there were no observers. They dispensed with the normal paraphernalia of spiritualist trance. There was no need for table rapping, amnesia, automatisms etc.. Often the pair would simply sit at a table, wherever they were. Yeats would then frame questions and George would discourse upon the subject. She would not pretend to be in a trance or speak in a funny voice like 'Is there anybody there?' This form of trance is one that we could all emulate - given enough practice. It is a more integrated approach, in which magick and one's ordinary life are less divided one from the other. Even the convention of using 'joined up' automatic script can be dispensed with given time. These things are *means to an end* not the end in itself. Once you understand the kind of awareness a trance is, you can often dispense with the trappings. This style of trancework or channeling is actually quite ancient and falls into a broad category of magick that is sometimes called the Apollonian style as opposed to the Dionysian system which is more energetic and exhausting.

Yeats asks in one of the trances, if any of his magical techniques, especially invocation, may be of use in analysis or for provoking the communicators. The answer is that he might use some variety of talismanic magick. The communicators' reply is thus:

'A symbol to be dipped in water after each night of sleep. Make a mantra over a small object give it to her to wear in sleep without saying what it is use(d) for. Charge with a simple clear image such as a flower.'

The purpose of this talisman is not necessarily to incubate a dream. It may indeed do that, but it may also serve to facilitate the next day's trance dialogue. When asked what image to put on the talisman the communicators reply:

'Use a nature symbol not a planetary one.'

At this stage in his life Yeats was, as the communicators reminded him, using his own words 'nothing but the embittered sun' His over intellectual, solar nature needed a counterbalance. Along with this the communicators say that he should *not* use a 'planetary' sigil, of the kind that would have been familiar to him from his work in the Hermetic Order of the Golden Dawn. He should instead use a more natural image, such as a flower. This could be a stylized drawing of a flower, like a sigil or rapid intuitive representation of a flower. I think it could be an actual flower or even the essence of a flower such as perfume oil.

The communicators say:

'Put the moving image on the object and don't do it again or you will gradually lose the first simplicity of the thought.'

This is so like the sigilisation technique of Austin Spare, it is uncanny.

I suggest it is a technique we could all try. I have done so now with success.


## Exercise 2

Step One: Take a piece of clean cartridge paper.

Step two: Make the mind calm, and in an intuitive flash mark it with a natural symbol, perhaps a flower or even dropping some perfume oil on the talisman.

Step three: say a mantramantra over it. Interesting that the communicators use the term 'mantra', a Sanskrit term and not the most obvious one. But it accords well with the decidedly eastern flavour of the 'Yeatsian' magical system.

Step four: Sleep with it under your pillow.

Step five: neutralize the talisman by emersion in water the next day

This is what happened to me on one of the occasion I did this: I smelt some rose oil, which is one of the most magical of oils; note the occurrence of this in the name Rosicrucian etc etc. I had the following dream:

## 13th November 1995

In the dream I went to a country estate, called either Grift or perhaps Drift farm. It had a grand house with a memorial column up high on one of the hills. On one of the tenant farms nearby, was a gorge with perhaps the disused entrance to a well shaft. The farmer had permission to excavate this shaft. There was some connection between this and a mutilated carving in a nearby church. The Jacobean carvings had been beheaded, and although the heads had been retrieved from various dealers, it had never been restored. There was something sinister about the family whose tomb it was. As we took away the rough course of blocks that hid the entrance to the well shaft, we found a much more elaborate tomb inside. There were artifacts scattered everywhere, including a fine blue ancient Egyptian perfume vial, the lid still intact. There was danger that our efforts would be too crude and that we would loose as much as we could salvage. Before I could stop them, someone rinsed the perfume bowl in water, leaving only a tiny trace of the original contents for analysis. I saw the name Francis Barrett, perhaps his hidden tomb. [The place of FB's burial is currently unknown although there have been reports of a tomb in Kensal Green cemetery.] I knew we would need more equipment now for properly documenting what we were finding. A dog appeared and was much attracted by the aroma coming from inside the still sealed tomb. And a local labourer was also drawn to the place.

There is a longer version of this piece in:

Tankhem: Seth & Egyptian Magick

Mandrake of Oxford, ISBN 1869928-865, 234pp, 12.99 (USD25)

# One Made for Exceptions Not for Laws:
# Wildean antinomianism in de Profundis

*Sven Davisson*

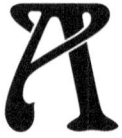

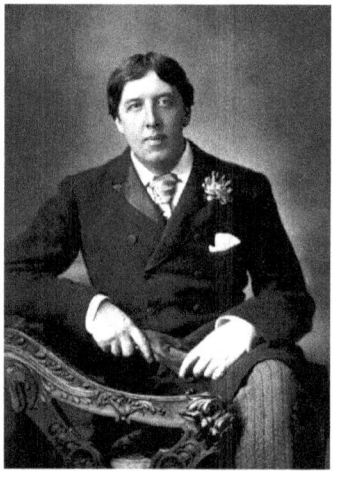

ntinomianism has diverse historical precedents and, one may suspect, reaches back to the first moral codes and religious strictures. Structured taboos and religious edicts have often give rise to counter-doctrines of transgression. This can be seen in certain Gnostic sects as well as the Tantrik practitioners of the *vama-marga*, or "Lefthand Path." Shri Mahendranath, last guru of the Nath line of Tantrism, describes the role of the seeker as based on amorality, "a path, way, or outlook which is neither moral nor immoral." (cited by Belarion, 19) The leader of a twentieth century Ophite-Cainite Gnostic church speaks of Carpocrates' theory of "salvation by reincarnatory fulfillment" as a notion "that if one does not commit some immoral act in *this* lifetime, he or she will likely commit it in the *next.*" (Belarion, 19)  In these doctrines it is the goal of the adept to reach a point that is beyond good and evil, free of social conditioning. For the adept to attain this higher vantage point, he or she must experience the evil as well as the good, for one cannot leave behind what one does not know.   One cannot truthfully reject what one has not experienced; rejection without experience is based on conditioning, not personal knowledge, and therefore can never be complete.

In *De Profundis* Wilde rejects morality, saying, "I am a born antinomian." (Wilde, 583).   In light of the spiritual nature underlying much of his work, it is certainly arguable that Wilde means here more than just simple moral transgression.  He appears to acknowledge a purpose within his antinomian stance.  In his piece "The Soul of Man Under Socialism," Wilde writes, "Disobedience… is man's original virtue."   In 1891, Wilde links disobedience with rebellion, but by the writing of *De Profundis*, he had given up rebellion as being too debilitating. In 1897, Wilde states, "He who is in a state of rebellion cannot receive grace," for "rebellion closes up the channels of the soul, and shuts out the airs of heaven." (Wilde, 595)  He sees antinomianism, then, as more than just rebelling against social norms; he is attempting to utilize his suffering and degradation for spiritual purpose.

Early in *De Profundis*, Wilde states "that the fools in the eyes of the gods and the fool in the eyes of man are very different."  He continues, "The real fool, such as the gods mock and mar, is he who does not know himself." (Wilde, 511)  Since the fool to the gods is one who lacks self-knowledge, it seems that Wilde is implying that the one who seeks to know himself is likely to be a fool to man.  Wilde is very careful to avoid entangling self-realization with a moral requirement for goodness.  At the root of his literary device, the transgressive paradox, resides a theory that one must know all sides of life to pass beyond their social definitions. He stresses the soul's ability to transform all that one does and experiences, even evil and suffering, into something right. "The supreme vice is shallowness. Everything that is realized is right." (Wilde, 511)

Wilde describes his friendship with Lord Alfred Douglas, "an unintellectual friendship, a friendship whose primary aim was not the creation and contemplation of beautiful things," for his fall from Art. (Wilde, 511) He blames his fall from the graces of proper society on his turning to that society to protect him— "The one disgraceful, unpardonable, and to all time contemptible action of my life was my allowing myself to be forced into appealing to Society for help and protection against [the Marquess of Queensberry]." (Wilde, 624) What most consider his true fall, making his name, as he says, "a low byword among low people," Wilde construes differently. (Wilde, 566) Wilde had used those acts hidden in the dark parts of London, as a means of stimulating his art and as a vantage point to look upon the Beautiful. He explains, "Tired of being on the heights I deliberately went to the depths in the search for new sensations. What the paradox was to me in the sphere of thought, perversity became to me in the sphere of passion."

Later in the work, he writes:

*People thought it dreadful of me to have entertained at dinner the evil things of life, and to have found pleasure in their company. But they, from the point of view through which I, as an artist in life, approached them, were delightfully suggestive and stimulating. It was like feasting with panthers. The danger was half the charm… They were to me the brightest of gilded snakes. Their poison was part of their perfection. (Wilde, 626)

The darker side of life, constructed by society as sinful, seems to have formed the grounding for Wilde's exalted privileging of Art and Beauty. He states this explicitly in this description of Dorian Gray, "There were moments when he looked on evil simply as a mode through which he could realize his conception of the beautiful." (Wilde, 305)

These three examples appear to hark toward a higher, more spiritual, definition of antinomianism.

What distinguishes Wilde's theory, of experiencing beauty through evil, from Lord Alfred's appetite-driven search for pleasure and Dorian's fall toward degradation is that Wilde sees in it a path toward realization. Wilde places his faith not in a higher power, but rather in the ability of the soul to transform actions. For Wilde the Soul is the ultimate spiritual alembic. In Wilde's opposition to denial he argues that the Soul "can transform into noble moods of thought, and passions of high import, what in itself is base, cruel, and degrading. (Wilde, 586) This reflects itself in the refrain of *De Profundis*, "The supreme vice is shallowness. Everything that is realized is right." (Wilde, 511) In Wildean morality there exists no pure evil; nothing one does or undergoes can be inherently bad. One always stands in relation to one's actions and possesses the ability to shape and reshape their reflexive meaning. Like his near contemporary, Nietzsche, Wilde levels out the constructed difference between good and evil and envisions a metaphysical space beyond their duality. In Wilde's cosmology the transformative capacity of the Soul is dependent on one's self-defined relation to one's actions. In *De Profundis*'s refrain "realized" is the key word—"Everything *realized* is right." (emphasis added)

Wilde places no emphasis on what is traditionally considered good or what is oppositionally conceived as evil. In his eyes, he sees that God, or the gods, do not distinguish between the two. "The gods are strange," Wilde writes. "It is not of our vices only they make instruments to scourge us. They bring us to ruin through what in us is good, gentle, humane, loving." (Wilde, 537) This sentiment is echoed later in the same text, and with more certitude, "I must accept the fact that one is punished for the good as well as for the evil that one does." (Wilde, 587) Wilde's acknowledgement that one is punished equally for all actions, regardless of their conventional definitions, does not lead him to a conclusion of nihilism. Surprisingly, it brings him instead toward a heightened, spiritually centered transcendence of the good/evil binary paradigm. For Wilde the gods indiscriminate punishment is not so strange after all. He actually possessed "no doubt that it is quite right one should be [for] it helps one, or should help one, to realize both, and not to be too conceited about either." (Wilde, 587) Here again Wilde places his importance on the act of "realizing." It is through the act of realization that the Soul becomes capable of transforming actions into deeper significances—a level where all conditioning, such as social constructions of good and evil, are removed or transfigured. For Wilde, "one only realizes one's soul by getting rid of all alien passions, all acquired culture, and all external possessions be they good or evil." (Wilde, 602) Wilde places this power of realization and the Soul in a concept of subjectivity and the seemingly paradoxical requirement of repentance.

When describing his philosophical outlook, Wilde adopts a skeptic's philosophical stance toward the notion of subjectivity: "I said in *Dorian Gray* that the great sins of the world take place in the brain, but it is in the brain that everything takes place." (Wilde, 609) As Wilde continues he could easily be paraphrasing from the dialogues of Sextus Empiricus or one of his successors. He bases his subjectivity on Sextus' argument of the senses, as he continues:

> We know not that we do not see with the eye or hear with the ear. They are merely channels for the transmission, adequate or inadequate, of sense-impressions. It is in the brain that the poppy is red, that the apple is odorous, that the skylark sings. (Wilde, 609)

From his theory of subjectivity, he posits his quest after "realization" internally. He writes, "If I may not find its secret within myself, I shall never find it." (Wilde, 584) The relation between Wilde's subjective self and the Soul's transformative capabilities is self-definitional. For Wilde, the act of repenting, or "realizing," one's actions is essential.

Though Wilde does not place a judgment on particular actions, he does make an important differentiation between various modes of relating to one's own actions. He argues "that there is nothing wrong in what one does," but "there is something wrong in what one becomes." (Wilde, 584) Wilde centers spiritual importance on a differentiation between one who remains in a singular realm of degradation, a slave to his appetites and drives (such as Lord Alfred), and the person who repents, thereby recognizing or "realizing" his actions. This separation is the crux of Wildean morality. "Of course the sinner must repent," Wilde states in *De Profundis*, "simply because otherwise he would be unable to realize what he had done. The moment of repentance is the moment of initiation." (Wilde, 616) Wilde's trial taught him, in retrospect, that it is not important to have one's actions recounted to one, or to be forced to confess them. In Wilde's conception, these are all spiritually meaningless. It is not what is said that is important, but that one says it oneself. Wilde defines "man's highest moment" as "when he kneels in the dust, and beats his breast, and tells all the sins of his life." (Wilde, 641) This marries nicely to *De Profundis*'s signature couplet; shallow people are the fools of the gods and it is the process of realization that distinguishes right from wrong.

When one looks at Wilde's own analysis of his scandalous fall, during and after his trials, one finds a developed cosmology based on antinomianism, transcendence, repentance and realization. Wilde's antinomianism is constituted in a knowledge of "evil" and "sin" based on a sense of active exploration, rather than passive acceptance of one's actions. He feels that "there is not a single degradation of the body which I must not try and make into a spiritualizing of the soul." (Wilde, 585) For Wilde amorality is both artistically and spiritually stimulating. Wilde relies on a subjective stance relative to good and evil, where antinomianism allows one to remove oneself from a position of moral conceit. Repentance is the fulcrum of Wilde's relativist morality. It is through the act of repentance that one realizes one's actions and can learn from them. Ultimately Wilde's philosophy is one of action— "people whose desire is solely for self-realization never know where they are going." (Wilde, 617) Wilde's understanding of antinomianism is based on a requirement to experience all sides of life, just as Wilde accepts the importance of suffering as well as pleasure, one must learn equality from good as well as evil.

### References:

Belarion [James M. Martin]. (1988) "Liber LXIX: On Sexual Antinomianism." Abrasax 1(1): 17-25.

Wilde, Oscar. *The Portable Oscar Wilde*. Richard Addington and Stanley Weintraub, editors. New York: Penguin, 1981.

## Ecclesia Gnostica Catholica

*Selections from Jules Stany Doinel*

### Première Homélie

(1890)


Sur La Sainte Gnose

À l'Église du Paraclet.


# I

Le nom de la sainte Gnose a été oublié parmi nous. La Gnose est l'histoire tragique de la chute de l'esprit dans la matière, et du voyage douloureux et providentiel que fait l'esprit pour remonter de la nuit du vide (le Kénôme) aux clartés du Plérôme divin, à la matière pleine d'illusions et de mirages de la paix souveraine et sacrée de l'idée pure, à cet abîme insondable de la Pensée, que, dans leur langage universel, expression d'une vérité unique, les philosophes ont nommé l'Absolu et les peuples ont appelé Dieu. Et pour opérer ce voyage et ce retour, odyssée de l'esprit humain, l'âme a deux ailes, la Science et l'Amour, le Christ céleste et le Saint-Esprit (Christos et Pneuma agion).

## II

Ces termes ne sauraient effrayer les Idéalistes, ni faire sourire les indifférents. Des âmes ont rompu ce pain et bu ce vin pendant des siècles. Quant aux matérialistes, esprits qui n'entrecroisent qu'une seule face des choses, la Gnose, peut leur citer ces paroles de Jean Scot Érigène: "Le danger n'est pas de chercher Dieu dans la nature, avec le flambeau du Logos; il est de s'obstiner à demeurer dans les limites de la nature, quand on est conduit au point où il faut les franchir." Scot pouvait parler ainsi, lui qui imposait deux sources à la Gnose: "la raison pure et la vision." Néanmoins les gnostiques sont bien éloignés de mépriser la science expérimentale mais ils pensent avec Plotin, avec les Oupanishads, qu'au-dessus du monde phénoménal, du monde de la Maïa, il y a la sphère de l'intelligible où les sens grossiers ne pénètrent pas. Ils savent qu'une idée qui se manifeste est une Théophonie, une apparition du Divin dans l'àme humaine, et que TEL DIEU SE RÉVÈLE, TEL IL EST ...

## III

La Gnose, c'est la science des Théophanies, des apparitions du Divin. C'est la science des Eons, ces théophanies sublimes, ces hypostases des perfections divines.

> Yeux ouverts du Seigneur sur l'ombre des déserts;
> Esprits qui remplisse l'air, la terre el les mers;
> Anges de tous les noms; mystérieux fantômes,
> Dont le monde invisible est plus plein que d'atomes;

Saints ministres du Père en tous les lieux vivant,

Qui luisez dans le feu, qui passez le vent,

Invisibles témoins de nos terrestres haines. **Lamartine**


Un jour, le grand Emmanuel Kant comparait l'âme qui plane dans l'Absolu à une colombe qui voudrait planer dans le vide. La Gnose, au contraire, nous enseigne et nous démontre que l'Absolu est l'atmosphère où se meut l'âme, puisque l'âme est une émanation de l'Absolu.

La Gnose, a dit Ephrem le Syrien, tresse une couronne à ceux qui l'aiment et elle les fait asseoir su un trône de Roi.

Et d'abord. quand le SEIGNEUR disait: "Je vou enverrai le Paraclet et il vous enseignera toute choses", il annonçait à la fois et la Gnose chrétienne et l'avènement du Saint-Esprit. À cette parole prophétique de Jésus, "la fleur des Éons", ont répondu, dans tous les temps, des initiateurs et des messager évangéliques. En feuilletant les apocryphes de la Bible, vous entendrez presque à chaque instant retentir la plainte de colombe de la sainte Gnose e son appel d'amour aux hommes qui ont faim et soif de la justice et de la vérité.


## IV


Jean nous a révélé qu'au commencement - dans le principe - le Logos fut émané par Dieu et que du Logos émanent la VÉRITÉ et la VIE. Le même Jean, dans l'Apocalypse, nous montre prophétiquement la nouvelle Jérusalem qui descend du sein de Dieu, parée comme une épouse pour son epoux. C'est la très sainte Gnose. C'est encore lui qui voit venir du ciel la femme symbolique, vêtue de soleil, couronnée de douze étoiles et ayant la Lune sous ses pieds. C'est lui enfin qui, dans son dernier chapitre, appelle l'époux au nom de l'épouse: Amen! Viens, Seigneur Jésus, viens!

C'est Paul parlant aux Colossiens de ce mystère de Dieu manifesté en Christos, dans lequel sont contenus tous les trésors de l'HYPERGNOSE - et, dans l'Épître aux Galates, disant: "Si vous êtes SOUS PNEUMA. VOUS n'êtes plus sous la Loi!" C'est Apollos, dans l'admirable Épître aux Hébreux, nous présentant le Fils, le MONOGÉNÈS héritier de toutes choses , par qui Dieu a fait les Eons: le Fils unique, splendeur de la Gloire et image empreinte de la SUBSTANCE divine, qui soutient toutes choses par le LOGOS.

## V

Les docteurs et les évêques de cette Gnose ont reçu en dépôt le sens ésotérique de la Bible. C'est à nous, pontifes selon l'ordre de Melchisédech, que les Anges ont confié le pectoral où flamboient l'Urim et le Thumim (Lévitique, viii, 8). C'est nous qui lisons dans le livre de la Loi (Néhémie, viii, 8). C'est notre écriture qui est cachetée au nom du Roi; c'est nous qui portons l'anneau du Roi (Esther, viii, 8).

C'est de nous qu'il est écrit: "Ceux qui sont revêtus de robes blanches, qui sont-ils et d'où sont-ils venus? Ce sont ceux qui ont souffert de la grande Tribulation et qui ont lavé leurs tuniques dans le sang spirituel de l'Agneau (Ram), et qui sont vierges des superstitions et des souillures du monde Hylique!"

La Gnose est l'essence même du Christianisme. (Comtesse d'Adhémar, Revue Théosophique, 21 juin 1889.) Voilà, nos bien-aimés, la plus juste définition du Gnosticisme. Or le Christianisme nous dit d'où nous venons et nous apprend où nous allons. Unde venis et quò vadis?

Savoir cela, c'est savoir la seule chose nécessaire. Porro unum est necessarium! Cette Gnose illuminative est la perle de l'Évangile pour laquelle l'Homme digne de ce nom doit vendre et donner tout ce qu'il a.

"Mon âme, d'où viens-tu? disait saint Basile. Qui t'a chargée de porter un cadavre? Si tu es quelque chose de ce céleste, ô mon âme! apprends-le-moi."

Et la Gnose répond: "En contemplant le Plérôme, tu connaîtras toutes choses."

## VI

L'illustre M. Franck, a justement remarqué que la Gnose prétend être une synthèse complète et définitive de toutes les croyances et de toutes les idées dont l'humanité a besoin pour so rendre compte de son origine, de son passé, de sa fin, de sa nature, de son avenir, des contradictions de l'nexistence et des problèmes de la vies, (Journal des Savants.)

Le premier Principe, c'est l'abîme, l'Unité absolue, existante par elle-même, le Père Ineffable, et qu'on ne peut définir justement parce qu'il est ineffable. C'est l'Être en puissance avec tous les possibles renfermées dans son sein, enveloppé dans son mystérieux silence (Sigê) et renfermant en soi l'Idée, l'Amour la Lumière et la Vie!

Si le Père Ineffable sort de ce Silence, si cet abîme déborde, si cette Puissance s'actionne, ce n'est pas la NÉCESSITÉ qui l'y contraint, c'est l'AMOUR. Et c'est parce qu'il aime qu'il se sépare de soi-même, se répand, se précipite, quitte sa solitude majestueuse, se prolonge pour aimer. Car, dit Valentin, il EST AMOUR, et il n'y a pas d'Amour sans objet aimé!

De cette unité d'amour jaillit la dualité (dyade), une dualité vivante, théophanie de l'Absolu, masculine et féminine, aimantée et aimée, et qui se révèle comme Esprit et Vérité (Nus et Alètheia).

# VII

Nous nous arrêterons ici, nos bien-aimés, remettant à une seconde Homélie épiscopale la suite de cette épopée sublime. Nous livrons ce préambule de la manifestation divine à vos méditations, à vos contemplations.

Vous qui faites partie de l'Église du Paraclet, unissez-vous à vos frères. C'est par vos prières et vos études, c'est, par votre obéissance à vos pasteurs invisibles, c'est par votre fuite de l'orgueil personnel et tout ce qui peut établir ou briser la charité, que vous réussirez à établir sur de fortes et profondes assises la communauté visible des Pneumatiques que les MANIFESTATIONS d'En-Haut nous annoncent et nous promettent. - Amen.

Donné sous le Thau, le 18 août 1890, neuvième année de Notre-Dame Saint-Esprit.

T JULES, évèque gnostique.

(JULES DOINEL).

## Première Homélie

On Holy Gnosis of the Church of Paraclet

*Translated by Sven Davisson*

## I

The name of the holy Gnosis has been forgotten among us. The Gnosis is the tragic history of the fall of spirit into matter, and of the painful and providential voyage of the spirit reascending to the night of the void (*Kénôme*) to the clarity of the divine Pleroma, but matter is filled with illusions and mirages of the sovereignty and sacredness of the pure idea, with the unfathonable abyss of Thought, that, in their universal language, expresses a single truth, that the philosophers named the Absolute and the people called God. And to facilitate this voyage and return, this odyssey of the human spirit, the heart has two wings, Science and Love, celestial Christ and the Holy Spirit (*Christos* and *Pneuma agion*).

## II

These terms do not frighten the Idealists, nor do they cause indifferent ones to smile. People of pure heart have broken this bread and drunk this wine for centuries. As for the materialists, spirits who intersect only one face of things, the Gnosis can quote to them these words of Jean Scot Érigène: *"the danger is not to seek God in nature, with the torch of the Logos; it is to obstinately remain oneself within the limits of nature, when one is lead to the point where they should be crossed."* Scott spoke of two sources of Gnosis: *"pure reason and vision."* Nevertheless the gnostics dismiss the scorn of experimental science, but they think with Plotin, with the Upanishads, that above the phenomenal world, the world of Maia, there is a sphere of comprehension where the coarse do not penetrate. They know that an idea which manifests is a Theophonie, an apparition of the Divine in the human soul, and that GOD REVEALS, THAT HE IS…

# III

Gnosis is the science of Théophanies, the manifestations of the Divine. It is the science of the Aeons, these sublime Théophanies, these hypostases of the divine perfections.

> The Lord opens his eyes on the shade of the deserts,
> Spirits which fill the air, the ground, the seas;
> Angels in all their names; mysterious phantoms,
> with which the invisible world is fuller than with atoms;
> Saintly Ministers of the Father living in all the places,
> Who shine in fire, who pass the wind,
> Invisible witnesses of our terrestrial hatreds. *Lamartine*

One day, the great Emmanuel Kant compared the spirit that resides in the Absolute with a dove that would like to live in the void. The Gnosis, on the contrary, teaches and shows us that the Absolute is the atmosphere where the spirit is drawn, since the spirit is an emanation of the Absolute. The Gnosis, says Ephrem the Syrian, braids a crown with those that like it and seats those that know on a King's throne.

And upon the arrival, when the LORD said: "I will send to you the Paraclet and he will teach you these things," He announced at the same time the Chrisitan Gnosis and the advent of the Holy Spirit. This prophetic word of Jesus, "the flower of the Aeons", answered, in all times, the initiator and the evangelic messenger. By dividing the apocryphal books of the Bible, you will almost understand at every instance the resounding lamentation of the dove of the holy Gnosis and its call of love for the men who are hungry and thirst for justice and the truth.

## IV

John revealed to us that at the beginning - in the principle - the Logos was emanated by God and the Logos emanated the TRUTH and LIFE. The same John, in the Apocalypse, prophetically shows us the new Jerusalem which descends from the centre of God, warded like a wife for her husband. It is the very holy Gnosis. It is still he who sees coming from the heavens the symbolic feminine, clad in the sun, crowned by twelve stars and having the Moon under her feet. It is he finally who, in its final chapter, calls the husband in the name of the wife: Amen! Come, Lord Jesus, come!

It is Paul speaking in Colossians about this mystery of God manifest in Christos, in which all the treasures of the HYPERGNOSIS are contained - and, in the Epistle in Galatians, saying: *"If you are UNDER THE PNEUMA. YOU are no more under the Law!"*[1] It is Apollos, in the admirable Epistle to the Hebrews, who introduces the Son, the MONOGÉNÈS heir to all things, for whom God made the Aeons: the unique Son, splendour of the Glory and impressive image of the divine SUBSTANCE, which supports all things by the LOGOS.

## V

The doctors and the bishops of this Gnosis received in deposit the esoteric meaning of the Bible. It is with us, pontiffs of the order of Melchisédech, that the Angels entrusted the breast-plate upon which the

---

[1] Galatians V, 18 "But if ye be led by the Spirit, ye are not under the law."

Urim and Thumim blaze (Leviticus,viii, 8).[2] It is we who read the book of the Law (Nehemiah, viii, 8).[3] It is our writing which is sealed in the name of the King; it is we who carry the ring of the King (Esther, viii, 8). [4] It is of us that it is written: *"Those which are covered by white robes, who are they and from where have they come? It is those who suffered from the great Tribulation and who washed their tunics in the spiritual blood of the Lamb (RAM), and who are superstitious virgins and stains of the Holy world!"* The Gnosis is the essence even of Christianity. (Countess of Adhémar, *Théosophique Review* , June 21, 1889.) Here are, our beloveds, the correct definition of Gnosticism. However Christianity speaks to us of where we come and teaches us where we go. *Unde venis et quò vadis?* To know that, is to know the only thing necessary. *Porro unum est necessarium!* This illuminating Gnosis is the pearl of gospel for which the Man worthy of this name must sell and give all that he has. *"My heart, from whence do you come?* holy Basile said. *Who charged you with carrying a corpse? If you are something of this celestial, O my heart! teach it to me."* And Gnosis answers: *"By contemplating the Plérôme, you will know all things."*

# VI

The illustrious Mr. Franck, correctly noted that the Gnosis claims to be a complete and final synthesis of all the beliefs and all the ideas which humanity needs to understand its origin, its past, its end, its nature, its future, contradictions of nonexistence and the problems of our lives. (*Journal des Savants*) The first Principle, it is the abyss, the absolute Unit,

[2] "And he put the breastplate upon him: also he put in the breastplate the Urim and the Thummim."

[3] "So they read in the book, in the law of God, distinctly, and gave the sense, and caused them to understand the reading."

[4] "Write ye also for the Jews, as it liketh you, in the king's name, and seal it with the king's ring: for the writing which is written in the king's name, and sealed with the king's ring, may no man reverse."

existing by itself, the Ineffable Father, and whom one cannot precisely define because it is ineffable. This Existence, in its power, contains all possible entities at its centre, wrapped in its mysterious silence (*Sigê*) and contains in itself the Thought, the Love, the Light and the Life! If the Ineffable Father leaves this Silence, if this abyss overflows, if this Power is actuated, it is not the NEED which it has constrained, it is the LOVE. And it is because he desires that he separates from himself, spreads himself, precipitates, leaves his majestic solitude, is prolonged for desire. Because, known as Valentine, it IS LOVE, and there is no Love without a desired object! Of this unit of love the duality (dyad) erupts, a duality alive, *théophanie* of the Absolute, male and female, magnetized and desired, and which appears like Spirit and Truth (*Nus* and *Alêtheia*).

## VII

We will stop here, our beloveds, giving in a second episcopal Homily the continuation of this sublime epic. We deliver this preamble of the divine demonstration for your meditations, for your contemplations. You who belong to the Church of Paraclet, join with your brothers. It is by your prayers and your studies, it is by your obedience to your invisible pastors, it is by your escape of personal pride and all that can establish or break charity, that you will succeed in establishing upon the powerful and profound assembly of the visible community of the Pneumatics[5] which the MANIFESTATIONS of the Most High announce and promise to us. - Amen.

Given under Thau, August 18, 1890, ninth year of Holy Spirit Our-Lady.

---

[5] Spiritual Beings, the highest of the three levels into which humanity is split.

# Rituel de la Fraction du Pain

## (1894)

Les Parfaits étant réunis, les femmes la tête couverte d'un voile blanc et les hommes ceints d'un cordon blanc, s'agenouillent et reçoivent la bénédiction de Sa Seigneurie, l'Évêque. Puis ils se relèvent et le choeur chante le cantique: Beati, vos AEones!

Sur la table drapée de lin, l'Évangile de Jean repose entre les deux flambeaux. L'Évêque et le diacre et la diaconesse assistants sont debout devant la table. Une fois le cantique achevé, Sa Seigneurie récite le Pater noster, en grec. L'Assemblée répond Amen.

Le diacre présente la coupe et le pain à l'Évêque. Le Prélat, revêtu de l'Étole (quand sa grâce le Patriarche officie, il est couvert du très auguste Pallium), élève les mains sur les espèces en disant: Eon Jesus prisquam pateretur mystice, accepit panem et vinum in stancias et venerabiles manus suas, et, elevatis oculis in coelum, fregit (l'Évêque rompt le pain), benedixit (l'Évêque forme le Tau sur le pain et la coupe) et dedit discipulis uais, dicens (Tout le monde se prosterne): Accipite et manducate et bibit omnes!

Le diacre portant le plateau et la diaconesse portant la coupe précèdent Sa Seigneurie qui s'avance vers les Parfaits. L'orgue joue une marche religieuse et lente.

L'Évêque, prenant le pain, l'élève au-dessus de l'assemblée en disant: ...

Puis il repose le pain sur le plateau, s'agenouille et adore.

Il se relève, prend la coupe et l'élève en disant: Calix meus inebrians quàm proeclaus est! - Calicem Salutaris accipiam et nomen Domini invocabo. -

Il s'agenouille et adore.

Il se relève, rompt un fragment du corps spirituel de Jésus et le mange. Il boit à la coupe du sang,

Pause. Orgues.

Il s'avance ensuite vers chaque Parfait et tend le pain et la coupe à chacun.

Silence. Orgues. - Adoration.

De retour à l'autel, l'Évêque étendant les mains dit: Que la grâce du très saint Plérôme soit toujours avec vous!

Les restes des espèces consacrées sont brûlés sur un réchaud, car le corps pneumatique du Seigneur ne doit pas être profané.

Après quoi, Sa Seigneurie donne la bénédiction gnostique et se retire entre les deux assistants qui portent les flambeaux.

# The Ritual of the Breaking of the Bread

*Translated by Sven Davisson*

The Perfect ones being joined together, the women the covered head of a white veil and the men girded with a white cord, kneel and receive the blessing of his Lordship, the Bishop. Then they rise and the choir sings the canticle: *Beati, vos AEones!*

On a table draped in linen, the Gospel of Jean rests between two tapers. The Bishop and the deacon and the deaconess assistants stand before the table. Once the canticle is completed, his Lordship recites the Pater noster, in Greek. The assembly answers: Amen.

The deacon presents the chalice and the bread to the Bishop. The Prelate, puts on the Stole (when his grace the Patriarch officiates, he is covered with very august Pallium), raises the hands over those present saying: *Eon Jesus prisquam pateretur mystice, accepit panem et vinum in stancias et venerabiles manus suas, et, elevatis oculis in coelum, fregit* (The Bishop breaks the bread), *benedixit* (The Bishop makes the shape of the Tau over the bread and the chalice) *et dedit discipulis uais, dicens* (All the world prostrates themselves): *Accipite et manducate et bibit omnes!*

The deacon carrying the paten and the deaconess carrying the chalice precede his Lordship who advances towards the Perfect ones. The organ plays a slow religious march .

The Bishop, taking the bread, raises it above the assembly while saying: *Calix meus inebrians quàm proeclaus est! Calicem Salutaris accipiam et nomen Domini invocabo.*

Then he puts the bread back onto the paten, kneels and adores.

He rises, takes the chalice and raises it while saying: *Calix meus inebrians quàm proeclaus est! Calicem Salutaris accipiam et nomen Domini invocabo.*

He kneels and adores.

He rises and brakes a fragment of the spiritual body of Jesus and eats it. He drinks from the cup of blood,

Pauses. Organ.

He then advances towards each Perfect one and offers the bread and the cup to each.

Silence. Organ. Adoration.

Upon returning to the altar, the Bishop extending his hands proclaims: May the grace of most holy Plérôme always be with you!

The remainder of the consecrated host are burned in the chafing-dish, for the pneumatic body of the Lord should not be profaned.

After which, his Lordship gives the gnostic benediction and withdraws between the two assistants who carry the tapers.

## Le Messe Noir

*J.K. Huysmans* from *La Bas (Down There)*

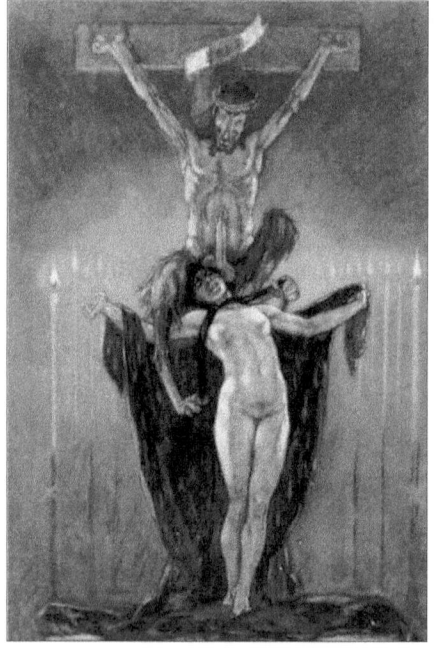

Felicien Rops

**J**n a fiacre they went up the rue de Vaugirard. Mme. Chantelouve was as in a shell and spoke not a word. Durtal looked closely at her when, as they passed a street lamp, a shaft of light played over her veil a moment, then winked out. She seemed agitated and nervous beneath her reserve. He took her hand. She did not withdraw it. He could feel the chill of it through her glove, and her blonde hair tonight seemed disordered, dry, and not so fine as usual.

"Nearly there?"

But in a low voice full of anguish she said, "Do not speak."

Bored by this taciturn, almost hostile tete-a-tete, he began to examine the route through the windows of the cab. The street stretched out interminable, already deserted, so badly paved that at every step the cab springs creaked. The lamp-posts were beginning to be further and further apart. The cab was approaching the ramparts.

"Singular itinerary," he murmured, troubled by the woman's cold, inscrutable reserve.

Abruptly the vehicle turned up a dark street, swung around, and stopped.

Hyacinthe got out. Waiting for the cabman to give him his change, Durtal inspected the lay of the land. They were in a sort of blind alley. Low houses, in which there was not a sign of life, bordered a lane that had no sidewalk. The pavement was like billows. Turning around, when the cab drove away, ht found himself confronted by a long high wall above which dry leaves rustled in the shadows. A little door with a square grating it was cut into the thick unlighted wall, which was seamed with fissures. Suddenly, further away, a ray of light shot out of a show window, and, doubtless attracted by the sound of the cab wheels, a man wearing the black apron of a wine shop keeper lounged through the shop door and spat on the threshold.

"This is the place'." said Mme. Chantelouve.

She rang. The grating opened. She raised her veil. A shaft of lantern light struck her full in the face, the door opened noiselessly, and they penetrated into a garden.

"Good evening, madame."

"Good evening, Marie. In the chapel?"

"Yes. Does madame wish me to guide her?"

"No, thanks."

The woman with the lantern scrutinized Durtal. He perceived, beneath a hood, wisps of grey hair falling in disorder over a wrinkled old

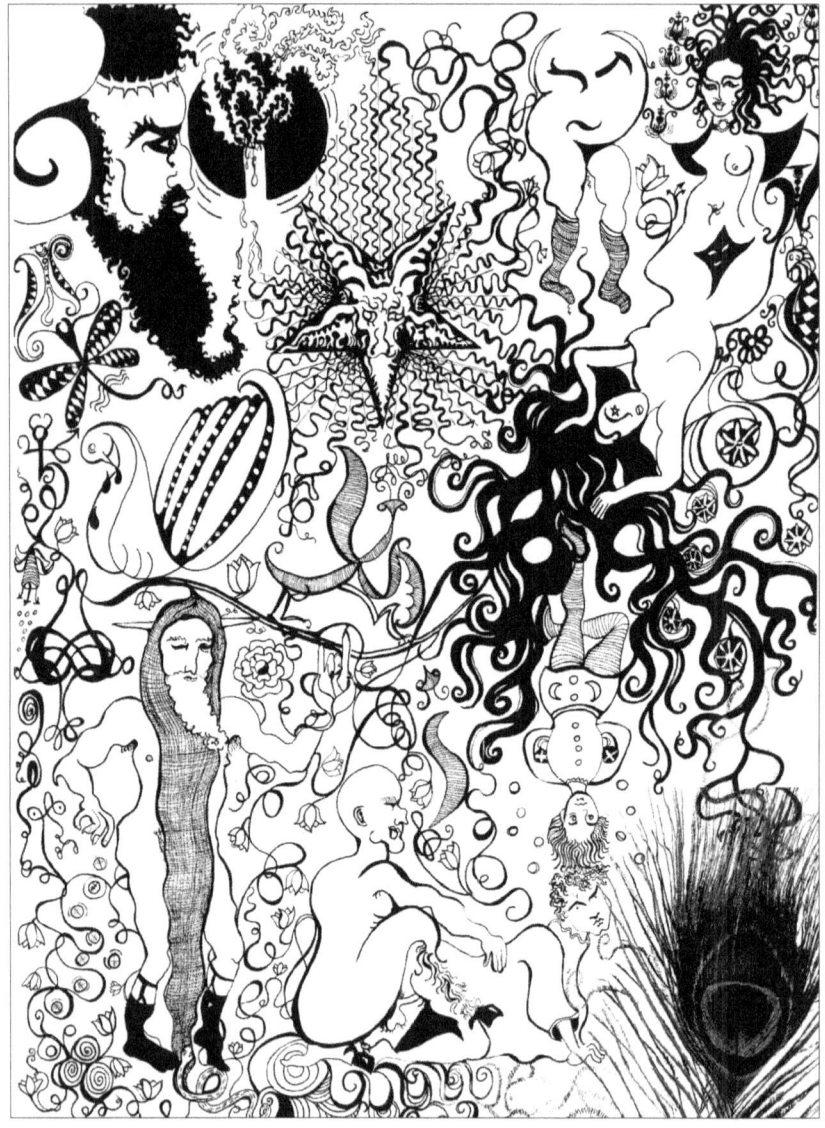

Eric K. Lerner

face, but she did not give him time to examine her and returned to a tent beside the wall serving her as a lodge.

He followed Hyacinthe, who traversed the dark lanes, between rows of palms, to the entrance of a building. She opened the doors as if she were quite at home, and her heels clicked resolutely on the flagstones.

"Be careful," she said, going through a vestibule. "There are three steps."

They came out into a court and stopped before an old house. She rang. A little man advanced, hiding his features, and greeted her in an affected, sing-song voice. She passed, saluting him, and Durtal brushed a fly-blown face, the eyes liquid, gummy, the cheeks plastered with cosmetics, the lips painted.

"I have stumbled into a lair of sodomists.—You didn't tell me that I was to be thrown into such company," he said to Hyacinthe, overtaking her at the turning of a corridor lighted by a lamp.

"Did you expect to meet saints here?"

She shrugged her shoulders and opened a door. They were in a chapel with a low ceiling crossed by beams gaudily painted with coal-tar pigment. The windows were hidden by great curtains. The walls were cracked and dingy. Durtal recoiled after a few steps. Gusts of humid, mouldy air and of that indescribable new-stove acridity poured out of the registers to mingle with an irritating odour of alkali, resin, and burnt herbs. He was choking, his temples throbbing.

He advanced groping, attempting to accustom his eyes to the half-darkness. The chapel was vaguely lighted by sanctuary lamps suspended from chandeliers of gilded bronze with pink glass pendants. Hyacinthe made him a sign to sit down, then she went over to a group of people sitting on divans in a dark corner. Rather vexed at being left here, away from the centre of activity, Durtal noticed that there were many women and few men present, but his efforts to discover their features were unavailing. As here and there a lamp swayed, he occasionally caught sight of a Junonian brunette, then of a smooth-shaven, melancholy man. He observed that the women were not chattering to each other. Their conversation seemed awed and grave. Not a laugh, not a raised voice, was heard, but an irresolute, furtive whispering, unaccompanied by gesture.

"Hmm," he said to himself. "It doesn't look as if Satan made his faithful happy."

A choirboy, clad in red, advanced to the end of the chapel and lighted a stand of candles. Then the altar became visible. It was an ordinary church altar on a tabernacle above which stood an infamous, derisive Christ. The head had been raised and the neck lengthened, and wrinkles, painted in the cheeks, transformed the grieving face to a bestial one twisted into a mean laugh. He was naked, and where the loincloth should have been, there was a virile member projecting from a bush of horsehair. In front of the tabernacle the chalice, covered with a pall, was placed. The choir boy folded the altar cloth, wiggled his haunches, stood tiptoe on one foot and flipped his arms as if to fly away like a cherub, on pretext of reaching up to light the black tapers whose odour of coal tar and pitch was now added to the pestilential smell of the stuffy room.

Durtal recognized beneath the red robe the "'fairy" who had guarded the chapel entrance, and he understood the role reserved for this man, whose sacrilegious nastiness was substituted for the purity of childhood acceptable to the Church.

Then another choir boy, more hideous yet, exhibited himself. Hollow chested, racked by coughs, withered, made up with white grease paint and vivid carmine, he hobbled about humming. He approached the tripods flanking the altar, stirred the smouldering incense pots and threw in leaves and chunks of resin.

Durtal was beginning to feel uncomfortable when Hyacinthe rejoined him. She excused herself for having left him by himself so long, invited him to change his place, and conducted him to a seat far in the rear, behind all the rows of chairs.

"This is a real chapel, isn't it?" he asked.

"Yes. This house, this church, the garden that we crossed, are the remains of an old Ursuline convent. For a long time this chapel was used to store hay. The house belonged to a livery-stable keeper, who sold it to that woman," and she pointed out a stout brunette of whom Durtal before had caught a fleeting glimpse.

"Is she married?"

"No. She is a former nun who was debauched long ago by Docre."

"Ah. And those gentlemen who seem to be hiding in the darkest places?"

"They are Satanists. There is one of them who was a professor in the School of Medicine. In his home he an oratorium where he prays to a 'statue of Venus Astarte mounted on an altar."

"No!"

"I mean it. He is getting old, and his demoniac orisons increase tenfold his forces, which he is using up with creatures of that sort," and with a gesture she indicated the choirboys.

"You guarantee the truth of this story?"

"You will find it narrated at great length in a religious" journal. Les annales de la saintete'. And though his identity was made pretty patent in the article, the man did not dare prosecute the editors. - What's the matter with you?" she asked, looking at him closely.

"I'm strangling. The odqur from those incense burners is unbearable."

"You will get used to it in a few seconds."

"But what do they burn that smells like that?"

"Asphalt from the street, leaves of henbane, datura, dried nightshade, and myrrh. These are perfumes delightful to Satan, our master." She spoke in that changed, guttural voice which had been hers at times when in bed with him. He looked her squarely in the face. She was pale, the lips pressed tight, the pluvious eyes blinking rapidly.

"Here he comes!" she murmured suddenly, while women in front of them scurried about or knelt in front of the chairs.

Preceded by the two choir boys the canon entered, wearing a scarlet bonnet from which two buffalo horns of red cloth protruded. Durtal examined him as he marched toward the altar. He was tall, but not well built, his bulging chest being out of proportion to the rest of his body. His peeled forehead made one continuous line with his straight nose. The lips and cheeks bristled with that kind of hard, clumpy beard which old priests have who' have always shaved themselves. The features were round and insinuating, the eyes, like apple pips, close together, phosphorescent. As a whole his face was evil and sly, but energetic, and the hard, fixed eyes were not the furtive, shifty orbs that Durtal had imagined.

The canon solemnly knelt before the altar, then mounted the steps and began to say mass. Durtal saw then that he had nothing on beneath his sacrificial habit. His black socks and his flesh bulging over the garters, attached high up on his legs, were plainly visible. The chasuble had the shape of an ordinary chasuble but was of the dark red colour of dried blood, and in the middle, in a triangle around which was an embroidered border of colchicum, savin, sorrel, and spurge, was the figure of a black billy-goat presenting his horns.

Docre made the genuflexions, the full- or half-length inclinations specified by the ritual. The kneeling choirboys sang the Latin responses in a crystalline voice which trilled on the ultimate syllables of the words.

"But it's a simple low mass," said Durtal to Mme. Chantelouve.

She shook her head. Indeed, at that moment the choir boys passed behind the altar and one of them brought back copper chafing-dishes, the other, censers, which they distributed to the congregation. All the women enveloped themselves in the smoke. Some held their heads right over the chafing-dishes and inhaled deeply, then, fainting, unlaced themselves, heaving raucous sighs.

The sacrifice ceased. The priest descended the steps backward, knelt on the last one, and in a sharp, tripidant voice cried:

"Master of Slanders, Dispenser of the benefits of crime, Administrator of sumptuous sins and great vices, Satan, thee we adore, reasonable God, just God!

"Superadmirable legate of false trances, thou receivest our beseeching tears; thou savest the honour of families by aborting wombs impregnated in the forgetfulness of the good orgasm; thou dost suggest to the mother the hastening of untimely birth, and thine obstetrics spares the still-born children the anguish of maturity, the contamination of original sin.

"Mainstay of the despairing Poor, Cordial of the Van-quished, it is thou who endowest them with hypocrisy, in-gratitude, and stiff-neckedness, that they may defend them-selves against the children of God, the Rich.

"Suzerain of Resentment, Accountant of Humiliations, Treasurer of old Hatreds, thou alone dost fertilize the brain of man whom injustice has crushed; thou breathest into him the idea of meditated vengeance, sure misdeeds; thou incitest him to murder; thou givest him the abundant joy of accomplished reprisals and permittest him to taste the intoxicating draught of the tears of which he is the cause.

"Hope of Virility, Anguish of the Empty Womb, thou dost not demand the bootless offering of chaste loins, thou dost not sing the praises of Lenten follies; thou alone receivest the carnal supplications and petitions of poor arid avaricious families. Thou determinest the mother to sell her daughter, to give her son; thou aidest sterile and reprobate loves; Guardian of strident Neuroses, Leaden Tower of Hysteria, bloody Vase of Rape!

"Master, thy faithful servants, on their knees, implore thee and supplicate thee to satisfy them when they wish the torture of all those who love them and aid them; they supplicate thee to assure them the joy of delectable misdeeds unknown to justice, spells whose unknown origin baffles the reason of man; they ask, finally, glory, riches, power, of thee, King of the Disinherited, Son who art to overthrow the inexorable Father !"

Then Docre rose, and erect, with arms outstretched, vociferated in a ringing voice of hate:

"And thou, thou whom, in my quality of priest, I force, whether thou wilt or no, to descend into this 'host, to in-carnate thyself in this bread, Jesus, Artisan of Hoaxes, Bandit of Homage, Robber of Affection, hear! Since the day when thou didst issue from the complaisant bowels of a Virgin, thou hast failed all thine engagements, belied all thy promises. Centuries have wept, awaiting thee, fugitive God, mute God I Thou wast to redeem man and thou hast not, thou wast to appear in thy glory, and thou sleepest. Go, lie, say to the wretch who appeals to thee, 'Hope, be patient, suffer; the hospital of souls will receive thee; the angels will assist thee; Heaven opens to thee.' Impostor I thou knowest well that the angels, disgusted at thine inert-ness, abandon thee! Thou wast to be the Interpreter of our plaints, the Chamberlain of our tears; thou wast to convey them to the Father and thou hast not done so, for this intercession would disturb thine eternal sleep of happy satiety.

"Thoti hast forgotten the poverty thou didst preach, enamoured vassal of Banksl Thou hast seen the weak crushed beneath the press of profit; thou hast heard the death rattle of the timid, paralyzed by famine, of women disembowelled for a bit of bread, and thou hast caused the Chancery of thy Simoniacs, thy commercial representatives, thy Popes, to answer by dilatory excuses and evasive promises, sacristy Shyster, huckster God!

"Master, whose inconceivable ferocity engenders life and inflicts it on the innocent whom thou darest damn - in the name of what original sin ?- - whom thou darest punish - by the virtue of what covenants ? - - we would have thee confess thine impudent cheats, thine inexpiable crimes! We would drive deeper the nails into thy hands, press down the crown of thorns upon thy brow, bring blood and water from the dry wounds of thy sides.

"And that we can and will do by violating the quietude of thy body, Profaner of ample vices, Abstractor of stupid purities, cursed Nazarene, do-nothing King, coward God!"

"Amen!" trilled the soprano voices of the choirboys.

Durtal listened in amazement to this torrent of blasphemies and insults. The foulness of the priest stupefied him. A silence succeeded the litany. The chapel was foggy with the smoke of the censers. The women, hitherto taciturn, flustered now, as, remounting the altar, the canon turned toward them and blessed them with his left hand in a sweeping gesture. And suddenly the choirboys tinkled the prayer bells.

It was a signal. The women fell to the carpet and writhed. One of them seemed to be worked by a spring. She threw herself prone and waved her legs in the air. Another, suddenly struck by a hideous strabism, clucked, then becoming tongue-tied stood with her mouth open, the tongue turned back, the tip cleaving to the palate. Another, in-flated, livid, her pupils dilated, lolled her head back over her shoulders, then jerked it brusquely erect and belaboured herself, tearing her breast with her nails. Another, sprawl-ing on her back, undid her skirts, drew forth a rag, enormous, meteorized; then her face twisted into a horrible grim-ace, and her tongue, which she could not control, stuck out, bitten at the edges, harrowed by red teeth, from a bloody mouth.

Suddenly Durtal rose, and now he heard and saw Docre distinctly.

Docre contemplated the Christ surmounting the taber-nacle, and with arms spread wide apart he spewed forth frightful insults, and, at the end of his forces, muttered the billingsgate of a drunken cabman. One of the choirboys knelt before him with his back toward the altar. A shudder ran around the priest's spine. In a solemn but jerky voice he said, "Hoc est enim corpus meum," then, instead of kneeling, after the consecration, before the preci-ous Body, he faced the congregation, and appeared tumefied, haggard, dripping with sweat. He staggered between the two choirboys, who, raising the chasuble, displayed his naked belly. Docre made a few passes and the host sailed, tainted and soiled, over the steps.

Durtal felt himself shudder.' A whirlwind of hysteria shook the room. While the choirboys sprinkled holy water on the pontiff's nakedness, women rushed upon the Eucharist and, groveling in front of the altar, clawed from the bread humid particles and drank and ate divine ordure.

Another woman, curled up over a crucifix, emitted a rending laugh, then cried to Docre, "Father, father!" A crone tore her hair, leapt, whirled around and around as on a pivot and fell over beside a young girl who, huddled to the wall, was writhing in convulsions, frothing at the mouth, weeping, and spiting out frightful blasphemies. And Durtal, terrified, saw through the fog the red horns of Docre, who, seated now, frothing with rage, was chewing up sacramental wafers, taking them out of his mouth, wiping himself with them, and distributing them to the women, who ground them underfoot, howling, or fell over each other struggling to get hold of them and violate them.

The place was simply a madhouse, a monstrous pandemonium of prostitutes and maniacs. Now, while the choirboys gave themselves to the men, and while the woman who owned the chapel, mounted the altar caught hold of the phallus of the Christ with one hand and with the other held a chalice between "His" naked legs, a little girl, who hither - to had not budged, suddenly bent over forward and howled, howled like a dog. Overcome with disgust, nearly asphyxiated, Durtal wanted to flee. He looked for Hyacinthe. She was no longer at his side. He finally caught sight of her close to the- canon and, stepping over the writhing bodies on the floor, he went to her. With quivering nostrils she was inhaling the effluvia of the perfumes and of the couples.

"The sabbatic odour!" she said to him between clenched teeth, in a strangled voice.

"Here, let's get out of this!"

She seemed to wake, hesitated a moment, then without answering she followed him. He elbowed his way through 'the crowd; jostling women whose protruding teeth were ready to bite. He pushed Mme. Chantelouve to the door, crossed the court, traversed the vestibule, and, finding the portress' lodge empty, he drew the cord and found himself in the street.

There he stopped and drew the fresh air deep into his lungs. Hyacinthe, motionless, dizzy, huddled to the wall away from him.

He looked at her. "Confess that you would like to go in there again."

"No." she said with an effort. "These scenes shatter me. I am in a daze. I must have a glass of water."

And she went up the street, leaning on him, straight to the wine shop, which was open. It was an ignoble lair, a little room with tables arid wooden benches, a zinc counter, cheap bar fixtures, and blue-stained wooden pitchers; in the ceiling a U-shaped gas bracket. Two pick-and-shovel labourers were playing cards. They turned around and laughed. The proprietor took the excessively short-stemmed pipe from his mouth and spat into the sawdust. He seemed not at all surprised to see this fashionably gowned woman in his dive. Durtal, who was watching him, thought he surprised an understanding look exchanged by the proprietor and the woman.

The proprietor lighted a candle and mumbled into Durtal's ear, "Monsieur, you can't drink here with these people watching. I'll take you to a room where you can be alone."

"Hmmm," said Durtal to Hyacinthe, who was penetrat-ing the mysteries of a spiral staircase, "A lot of fuss for a glass of water!"

But she had already entered a musty room. The paper was peeling from the walls, which were nearly covered with pictures torn out of illustrated weeklies and tacked up with hairpins. The floor was all in pieces. There were a wooden bed without any curtains, a chamber pot with a piece broken out of the side, a wash bowl and two chairs.

The man brought a decanter of gin, a large one of water, some sugar, and glasses, then went downstairs.

Her eyes were sombre, mad. She enlaced Durtal.

"No!" he shouted, furious at having fallen into this trap. "I've had enough of that. It's late. Your husband is waiting for you. It's time for you to go back to him - - "

She did not even hear him.

"I want you," she said, and she took him treacherously and obliged him to desire her. She disrobed, threw her skits on the floor, opened wide the abominable couch, and raising her chemise in the back she rubbed her spine up and down over the coarse grain of the sheets. A look of swooning ecstasy was in her eyes and a smile of joy on her lips.

She seized him, and, with ghoulish fury, dragged him into obscenities of whose existence he had never dreamed. Suddenly, when he was able to escape, he shuddered, for he perceived that the bed was strewn with fragments of hosts.

"Oh, you fill me with horror! Dress, and let's get out of here."

While, with a faraway look in her eyes, she was silently putting on her clothes, he sat down on a chair. The fetidness of the room nauseated him. Then, too-he was not absolutely convinced of Transubstantiation-he did not believe very firmly that the Saviour resided in that soiled bread - but - In spite of himself, the sacrilege he had in-voluntarily participated in saddened him.

"Suppose it were true," he said to himself, "that the Presence were real, as Hyacinthe and that miserable priest at test — No, decidedly, I have had enough. I am through. The occasion is timely for me to break with this creature whom from our very first interview I have only tolerated, and I'm going to seize the opportunity."

Below, in the dive, he had to face the knowing smiles of the labourers. He paid, and without waiting for his change, he fled. They reached the rue de Vaugirard and he hailed a cab.

As they were whirled along they sat lost in their thoughts, not looking at each other.

"Soon?" asked Mme. Chantelouve, in an almost timid tone when he left her at her door.

"No," he answered. "We have nothing in common. You wish everything and I wish nothing. Better break. We might drag out our relation, but it would finally terminate in recrimination and bitterness. Oh, and then-after what happened this evening, no I Understand me? No!"

And he gave the cabman his address and huddled himself into the furthest corner of the fiacre.

# Tarot Reviews

*Eric K. Lerner*

**The Mystical Origins of the Tarot:**
**From Ancient Roots to Modern usage,** Paul Huson
(Destiny Books, 2004, 352pp, $18.95)

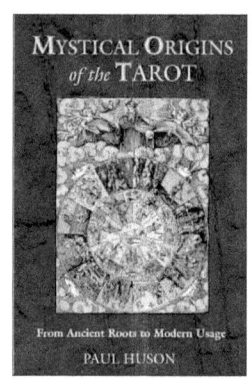

The title of Paul Huson's *Mystical Origins of the Tarot* is misleading. It implies that the author advocates that tarot is a transmittal of esoteric knowledge. This notion has long been popular in the tarot community going back to the 1700's when Court de Gebelin and Alliette stated that Tarot represented the secret occult wisdom of the ancient Egyptians. Huson eschews such interpretations about tarot's origin. Instead, he identifies precise sources for the cards. He describes influences that were being brought to bear in the late Middle Ages when the first Tarots were painted for noble Italian families.

One notable departure Huson makes from how others have tried to explain Tarot origins is that he begins his study with the 56 small cards, rather than the 22 major arcana. Historical evidence suggests that the pips were created first. The most complete example of an early 56-card deck is the fifteenth century Malmuk playing cards. However, there are examples of individual cards that date back more than three centuries earlier to the Arab world. He persuasively argues that Malmuk's four suits are derived from ancient Persia's caste system that included Magi, Kings and warriors, farmers and artisans, and those who would serve the rest. These can be likened to both the four cardinal virtues and the four card suits: Cups, Coins, Polo sticks and Swords. His analysis takes the reader through Medieval Arabic trading routes to Southern Europe. The cross-cultural designations of class systems, values and religious beliefs were reflected in the card games people played. The playing card suits evolved as documentation of Persian, Arabic and eventually European economic and moral norms.

Huson then explores how the trumps correspond to aspects of Medieval Theatre. Early drama consisted of morality, mystery, danse macabre and miracle plays. The plays provided the Church (the governing power body) with a means of indoctrinating the largely illiterate public. Early tarot artists depicted actors and scenes from these familiar entertainments. For instance, Huson shows how the sixth trump, the lovers, depicts the Youth and Maiden from the Danse Macabre plays. The Maiden and the Youth were akin to popular movie and television stars of our day. They were faces that the public would instantly recognize. Huson traces similar sources for each of the major arcana to the old spectacles. His argument is persuasive. The major arcana documented familiar cultural icons, and could have been construed to have the same edifying value as the plays in which they appeared.

Next Huson looks at the history of card divination. He illustrates the use of cards as prognostication tools developed from sortilege and oracular books in the 15th century. These were precursors to tarots first being used in fortune telling around 1750. He provides us with a succinct portrait of Alliette. Also known as Etteilla, Alliette linked his tarots to initiatory wisdom of ancient Egypt. This helped popularize belief that tarots were powerful oracles. Huson steers clear of validating Alliette's mystical claims. Rather he focuses on Alliette's very real contribution of cartomantic meanings that endure today and chronicles how tarot meanings have evolved. He includes the contributions of Alliette, Papus (Gerard Encausse), Eliphas Levi (and the introduction of qabalistic symbolism), the Golden Dawn, and A.E. Waite. Huson also brings to light the important role that the Picatrix, an Arabic grimoire with its descriptions of the 36 astrological decans, played in how the Golden Dawn applied decan attributes to the pip cards.

One omission on Huson's part seems to be the contribution of Oswald Wirth. Even though Wirth did not publish his study, Tarot of the Magicians, until 1926, his rectified Tarot first appeared in the 1880's. It was cited by Papus in *Tarot of the Bohemians* and exhibited an important influence on the creation of the Waite-Smith Tarot. Wirth synthesized alchemical, qabalistic and astrological meanings into Tarot and lucidly developed the theories of both Papus and Levi. (Please note: one of the characters in J.K. Huysmans *La Bas*, which is sampled elsewhere in this issue, is either based on Wirth or is a synthesis of Wirth and his dear friend Stanislaus de Gautia.) That omission seemed unusual to me. Perhaps it is because the majority of Wirth's theories relate to only the Major Arcana.

In spite of that, *The Mystical Origins of the Tarot* stands out as a supremely useful reference book. Huson presents the evolution of meanings for each card in a straight forward manner and includes his own suggested interpretations. By presenting the different interpretations side by side, the reader is encouraged to compare and contrast the interpretations and make his own call.

Huson also offers solid advice on reading technique. Of particular value is that he explains how to develop sentence strings from tarots. To develop a coherent narrative or logical argument from a spread or sequence of cards is critical to a valid and accessible reading. I appreciated seeing someone with a sharp intellect explain how to do this and provide examples.

As many of you know, I made my living for most of the past five years reading tarot for people. I believe my reaction to this book may be useful to others who might consider reading it. There are points on which I differ with Huson. I prefer to read the Thoth deck, and I tend to closely follow Crowley's interpretations. These do not employ reversals (a concept that Huson does use) and instead rely on elemental harmonies to determine the orientation of a card. In addition, the Thoth deck synthesizes Golden Dawn interpretations with other occult beliefs in framing a card's basic statement. That deck has worked for me. However, I enjoyed having some of my fundamental views challenged by Huson. His approach to actual meaning is a lot more down to earth than many of the "new age" texts on tarot. That helped open me to the possibility of meanings for the cards that have stood the test of history, yet seemed new to me in context of meanings I've long used.

The bottom line is that any technician stands to improve his work by having his conceptions challenged. It simply keeps you on your toes. The fact that Huson looks for lucid interpretations based on historical precedent goes a long way to bringing tarot down to earth. That stands to make it useful. Any form of occultism, spirituality or magick is beyond useless if it does not provide its practitioners and clients a true means of enhancement. Most shamans and dedicated occult practitioners are very good technicians. Even though the purpose of their exercises may be spiritual, their approaches to work are very practical and matter of fact. It is this type of pragmatism that provides a solid platform for mystical evolution. You cannot begin a journey unless your feet are on terra firma on some level. Huson by being clear eyed in his approach to tarot provides a worthy foundation from which one can begin a journey toward higher truth. Ironically, his lucid scholarship in *The Mystical Origins of Tarot* may truly provide a mechanism for mystical levels of attainment for his readers.

## Deck Roundup

The past thirty years has seen an explosion in the number of tarot decks available. They seem as numerous as comic books, and like that genre they embody pearls and scum. I hate to waste my time in muck. Plus, since I've been known to create the odd deck myself, my sense of fair play dictates that I limit myself to those decks I like, or at least those for which I can offer what I hope is constructive criticism.

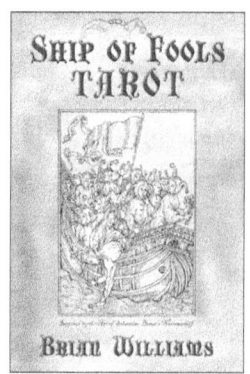

I wish to start with a deck/book set that was published posthumously: *Ship of Fools Tarot* by Brian Williams from Llewellyn. Williams was one of the few true American Taroists. He died in early 2002 after a long battle with cancer. Starting in 1987, with the Renaissance Tarot, Williams created five deck/book sets. (He also wrote the text for the book accompanying the *Light and Shadow Tarot*.) His *Po Mo Tarot* is a send up of both tarots and Modern art that's well worth scoring on EBay since it is sadly out of print. Even though he would emerge as a very serious tarot scholar, that deck best exhibited his sharp wit and love of art. In it he steered clear of lofty pretensions. However, Williams was a serious scholar of the Renaissance and Italy. He resurrected interest in the 97 card Minchiate style decks. This type of deck includes the horoscope signs, four virtues, four elements and a "Fame" card in addition to the traditional 78 cards. In his research on the Minchiate, Williams developed the theory that the traditional elemental associations and meanings for suits Swords and Staves (Wands) should be reversed. In other words, Swords are traditionally associated with Air (Sanguine Temperament) and Staves with Fire (Choleric Temperament.) His argument that appears in Destiny Books' *Minchiate Tarot* is worth reading.

The inversion of elemental affinities between the two suits is something Williams continues to advocate in *The Ship of Fools Tarot*. God forbid we have evidence of someone consistently sticking by his intellectual convictions! Let's look at his last creative endeavor. *The Ship of Fools Tarot* is based on early Renaissance literary classic *Das Narrenshichiff* (Ship of Fools) by Sebastian Brant. The work is a poetic satire surveying human folly. The fact that many of the woodcuts illustrating his tome were created by a young Albrecht Durer didn't exactly hurt the integrity of the text. *The Ship of Fools* fulfills many of the criteria Huson ascribes to the twenty-two major arcana in reflecting iconography familiar to Renaissance audiences through contemporary morality plays. Williams himself notes in the introduction to the accompanying book that he had cited *Das Narrenschiff* in some of his examinations of imagery that contributed to early tarot.

The deck's concept is that each card features at least one fool. Given the popularity of the contemporary notion that the twenty-two arcana represent an archetypal fool's journey, executing a deck in such a manner seems like an obvious approach. The cards' images are based on illustrations appearing in *Das Narrenschiff*. Some are clones of the original woodcuts, although Williams's signature clean linear style of pen work is obvious to the trained eye. Others combine elements from the *Narrenshiff* illustrations with design elements from the Marseilles and Waite-Smith tarots. Williams's text carefully explains all of his visual sources. To a tarot nut like yours' truly I really find that quite fascinating.

I really enjoy this deck and accompanying book. Face it: *The Ship of Fools Tarot* introduces many readers to a literary classic and provides thoughtful insights about consistent archetypes of the human imagination. Plus, it's tongue in cheek. Williams obviously had fun with this and didn't mind including the audience in the banter. What makes this credible is that he does so while strictly adhering to Tarot convention. He does not create new suits or introduce new fangle arcana. He understands the conventions of tarot as genre and fits his observations as well as winks and nods within its established structure.

Because of its value as literary criticism and education and its adherence to tarot standards, I'm reluctant to say this is not a good choice for a first deck. An aspiring reader can do a lot worse than to develop a perspective on divination based on the work of Brant and Williams. Developing a sense of humor doesn't hurt either. The cards fit well in my hand. The monochrome sepia ink works for me. It lends the images warmth and helps convey a sense of history and thus the timelessness of human folly and existence. I also appreciate it when an American artist and publisher take a risk on a tarot deck that assumes its audience is intelligent and capable of expanding its knowledge base. Examining this deck has been a worthwhile investment of time. *The Ship of Fools Tarot* may indeed prove to be a source to which I return for inspiration.

Tarot has emerged as a unique artistic and literary genre, but it should not be thought of purely as an intellectual exercise. Its primary application is divination. It is not meant to be an art appreciation primer. I've been very kind to Williams' *Ship of Fools Tarot* because that deck meets a very difficult test. It succeeds in being intellectually stimulating while rigorously obeying the tenants of tarot. However, there are experiments that are much farther flung than that. Many of these appear as Art Tarot—that is a tarot presented as a unique statement of an artist creator. The best known of these is probably Dali's Tarot due to the prestige of the artist himself. I must confess that for a long time I would not touch that deck with a ten-foot pole. It was not because I have anything against Dali per se, but we have been deluged with endless imitations of that deck in the form of collage decks created by anyone who got hold of a pair of scissors, old magazines and card stock. Many of these efforts were not the result of an understanding of tarot. They were onanistic exercises is self-congratulation. Recently, I broke down and acquired a copy of Dali's deck, and was shocked to discover that it's a quite fine deck. I guess when you think of the atrocities committed in the names of Jesus Christ and Allah, you can forgive an artist if his inspiration has been imitated by a bunch of idiots.

That still leaves us with challenge levied by this whole art tarot genre. How should they be judged? I have yet to develop a consistent answer. Any artistic genre has to be open to experimentation in order to expand its horizons. However, tarot is first a practical tool. I admit I'd rather see a bad art tarot than another flowery recreation of the Waite-Smith deck.

As "art" tarot offerings, let us examine *Tarot of the Imagination* by Pietro Alligo (author) and Ferenc Pinter (artist) and the *Dante Tarot* by Giordano Bertis (author) and Andrea Serio (artist), both from the Italian publisher LoScarbeo and available stateside through Llewellyn. Over the years LoScarbeo has produced tarots of both innovation and idiocy. It has taken some chances. If you as a publisher, or artist for 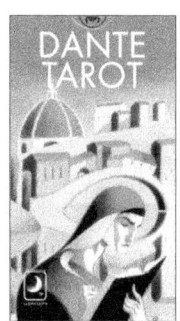 that matter, are going to hit pay dirt in art, caution to the wind is not the worst course. Lo Scarbeo has kept some good artists in Chianti and pasta. And it has provided many valuable reprints of historical decks too.

The first for discussion is *Tarot of the Imagination*, which is based on the notion that history has provided mankind with common visual references. Hence, each individual will have a reaction to seeing an image of a Nazi soldier. The knee-jerk associations with Nazism may be challenged if that soldier is seen innocently flirting with a pretty girl in front of the Eiffel tower. What do you think that means? Is it danger? Could the girl be a partisan with a stiletto strapped to her garter belt? Or maybe they're just two young people independent of their historical associations doing what comes naturally on a beautiful spring day? If this type of ratiocination intrigues you, you will probably enjoy *Tarot of the Imagination.*

I believe that it is the visual stimulation of the card that ultimately triggers visionary experience. A tarot image that yields new details upon successive viewing has a great deal of use as an oracle. Ferenc's artwork is realistic in physical detail with occasional forays into surrealism. The colors are muted and there are few hard lines in any of the paintings. This gives the iconography a hazy dreamlike quality consistent with the stated intention of the deck to reflect imaginative faculty.

How does this deck stand up to the criteria I applied to *Tarot of Fools*? This is where the going gets difficult. In the major arcana, Pinter stays within the bounds of standard iconography. Albeit he mixes historical epochs, but any who has ever read a Marseilles deck should be able to figure out what's going on.

The minor arcana are more troubling. Now, the purpose of the deck seems to be to provoke visceral response that require thought and insight to analyze and hence draw valid conclusions about the questions at hand. Over the years consistent meanings for minor arcana have been established through keys provided by sources such as Alliette (Ettiella), the Golden Dawn, qabalah, Waite (and Crowley.) I have some difficulty in identifying which if any of those keys Pinter consistently uses. To test this, I arbitrarily pulled the Four of Swords. The image shows the back of a Solider, probably a nazi, brandishing a machine gun with six people lined up against what appears to be a broken wall. There is a blaze of white on either side of the soldiers' head that may be smoke. Something ominous is going on here. A few of the lined up figures are very casual in their physical attitudes. What are the common divinatory meanings for the Four of Swords? Let's turn to Huson's very useful reference book. He cites Etteilla leaning toward interpretations in line with either solitude or wise administration or circumspection; Mathers similarly with Solitude, abandonment, precaution or retreat; Golden Dawn Lord of Rest from Strife, Peace from and after war, possible abundance; Waite: vigilance, retreat, possibly tomb and exile, although possibly salvaged by wise administration. That leaves the Picatrix and its assignations for the planetary decans that are often correlated to the tarot pips. The applicable meaning of the 21st to 3oth degree of Libra ruled by Jupiter according to Huson is ill deeds (traditional vices). That seems the closest of traditional sources, albeit a stretch, to what is suggested by the image. However, the supporting key word sheet provided by Lo Scarbeo says, "Massacre. Nobody looked them in the face or asked their names." That statement is certainly consistent with the impact the image had on me, but where does that emerge from the common understandings of tarot? Perhaps that can be construed as ill dignified interpretation of Crowley-Harris Four of Swords, Truce. However, the creators do not consistently adhere to Crowley's logic elsewhere.

Of course, such an image is consistent with common human experience. But I have to wonder why the artist did not more precisely correlate his iconography to traditional tarot meanings. Certainly, such an image of capricious cruelty could fit with many other of the pips in the suit of swords. Certainly the Eight of Swords readily comes to mind. In case of that card the Imagination image is more consistent with the traditional dread associated with it. It displays the image of a partisan carrying what appears to be a fallen comrade (or victim) slung over his shoulder. The meaning described in the key is Sacrifice. Misfortune is rife in the interpretations of the Eight of Swords. However, I believe that sacrifice is en-nobling. It means to make sacred. And I have not typically encountered anything noble in other interpretations of the Eight of Swords.

Now where does this lack of a proven system of cartomantic meaning place *Tarot of the Imagination?* Ferenc uses visceral images. Many defy simple black and white explanations. It takes courage to do that. Obviously, the artist committed himself to doing a series of paintings that stimulate us to think based on our understanding of history and common experience. I wish he had studied his divinatory meanings of the pips more closely. That could have seriously enhanced the enduring value of this deck.

Still, I responded to this deck. The way it comes packaged seems willy-nilly. It is not organized by number, suit or division of minor arcana from major arcana. Typically decks come organized numerically by suit with the major arcana separate from the minor arcana. In *Tarot of the Imagination*, pips of different suits and Major arcana were intermixed. That made me immediately question whether or not the artist was making a significant statement through the ordering of the cards, as they appear fresh out of the box. At this point, I feel that the purpose of the arbitrary arrangement is a statement about human perception itself. We analyze data in a collage manner. Hence, many artists argue that collage is the logical medium for this epoch. We watch news reports about tsunamis one moment and flipping through sports programs and old movies the next. We experience our world in little chunks. That is also one of the significant underlying statements of Tarot of the Imagination. The deck did make me think about perception. Some of the images are especially strong. Certainly, one can gain a deeper appreciation for life and art through looking at the deck.

*The Dante Tarot* is both more troubling and delightful that *Tarot of the Imagination*. The deck was developed to reflect the worldview of Dante whose writing predates Tarot. Dante passed away in 1321. It was not until the next century that there is evidence that the 22 major arcana were added to the Malmuk playing cards, giving birth to a 78-card tarot. Using more ancient historical sources as inspiration for tarot art is a very old practice. Early Tarots included images of Greek gods and Mesopotamian Kings. And of course ancient Egypt has continued to be a visual reference for a large number of Tarots. Dante's work was far-reaching, cosmic and iconographic in nature. It makes a good source of inspiration for Tarot. Giordano Berti states that he wanted to base the deck's Trumps on Dante's work *Convivio*, an encyclopedia of medieval knowledge. Only Trumps 11 and 13 through 15 retain the names of the traditional arcana. For instance the trump occupying the role and place of The Fool is called Necessity and the Empress Knowledge. However, the artist Andrea Serio retains visual keys for the trumps based on established Tarot conventions. The Figure in Necessity is obviously a vagabond with a dog at his heels as Fool is most often depicted. Knowledge is a powerful woman obviously adept in the mysteries of sexual knowledge and morality, an Empress.

Serio's artwork is what made me want to acquire this deck. He uses pastels for the work that evoke the exaggerated geometric style seen in much PostModern Italian art. The choice of pastels imparts a sensual flowing quality to the contours. His background according to the deck's liner notes is in comics. That serves him very well, because he is able to convey a dynamic narrative in his compositions. Like the best comic art, the images talk and communicate essential information elegantly. In light of the quality of the art, I am a bit reluctant to give the deck anything but praise. The artwork can be contrasted with that in *Tarot of the Imagination*. Serio clearly defines what is going on in his compositions. Even though Ferenc is more realistic in drawing style, there is a lot more ambiguity in his compositions. It seems ironic that Serio with a more abstract manner of characterization should be more lucid. But his images are more strictly composed in their manipulation of space. Consistently, he centers his principle actors. Frequently the figures occupying the first or third sections of the composition relate to the key actor in a chronological manner. For instance in the Necessity (Fool) image, the central figure is walking away from a group of three men (one is pointing at him). One gets the clear impression that these represent rational forces in Society. They stand against pillars, buildings that echo ancient Greek architecture. The figure's head, hand and the front half of his dog appear in the final third of the composition. This indicates that he is departing for a less structured feral environment. It is interesting that Serio chooses to distort the human form so that the head is not centered over the body. He uses the composition to make the statement that the traveler is leaving behind logic to such an extreme that his own mind is not centered, as it should be physically. It is the consistent use of dramatic composition that makes the images talk.

The relationship to traditional tarot *The Dante Tarot* is further strained by the creation of new suits: Bricks, Flames, Clouds and Lights. Bricks seem to correspond to pentacles or disks since they deal with material situations in Dante Aligheiri's life. Interestingly, he writes that Flames fulfill the function of Swords and Clouds of Wands. This is similar to Williams's interpretation of the elemental affinities of these suits. Lights take the place of water. There is no consistent rationale for what the pips mean in relationship to popular tarot interpretations. A simple example is the Two of lights. Virtually every interpretation of the Two of Cups deals with the realization of Love. Generally, it's one of the happier cards you can draw unless ill dignified. In the Dante Tarot, the cheat sheet states: "Heavens of the Moon. Changes underway. Futile Hopes. Unthinkable results." The image depicts two women in a dreamy moonlit grove. A handmaid is delivering a message to her Queen. The Queen's sense of anticipation and dignity are both indicated by the subtle prayer-like position of her hands. Again, Serio does an excellent job of conveying the author's intended meaning and managed to take it a level deeper through the grace of his execution. However, does the intellectual vigor of this endeavor really match what Williams does with his medieval source in Tarot of Fools?

The bottom line is that if you like art tarot at all, you are going to buy this deck. I realize that the author's intention is to pay tribute to one of the world's great authors, and he may have felt at odds trying to fit Dante's precepts into the constructs of cartomantic meanings generally attributed to Tarot. If they had called this The Dante Oracle rather than the Dante Tarot, I'd probably be a lot more comfortable.

If Tarot is going to get the respect I believe it richly deserves as an artistic genre, there must be a consistent litmus. Both these tarots from Lo Scarbeo challenge this litmus. I wish the authors had done a little more to convince me that they had paid attention to what boundaries they were pushing though demonstrating more attention to what they were stating in regard to the divinatory meanings of the pips. Finally, I sincerely hope that Serio does more tarots. His ability to create images that are both aesthetically pleasing and meaningful is quite welcome. He possesses an outstanding narrative feel that he expresses in his tarots. I have not really seen that in a tarot artist since Elisabetta Cassari had her heyday with the bracing series of tarots she created for Solleone in the late Eighties. (Her work provides an excellent example of an artist who could turn traditional tarot meanings on their ears and spin them around a few times. Yet, you knew this lady had done her homework and was using her effrontery to fashion a cynical and dark worldview. Recent history has done a good job of proving her correct. Visionary potential is part of the tarot experience, right?) I'd like to see in what direction Serio goes.

*The Tarot of the Elements* by Isha Lerner and Amy Ericksen struck an immediate chord with me through the immediate "primitive" quality of its artwork. (I admit that it also caught my eye that my full name is spelled out on the box Isha LERNER AmyERICKsen.) The deck's imagery is based on the visual expressions of shamanistic cultures, ranging from cave paintings to Afrikan and Native American art. I believe that this type of iconography is closest to both the conscious and subconscious expression of man. The visionaries responsible for those fundamental creations expressed themselves in a most immediate manner, not defined or constrained by a need for the logic of language. Therefore, work that incorporates these primary sources may well strike an immediate response with most viewers. Given that I myself have looked to these sources in particular for my own understanding of existence and inspiration, I perceive immediate correspondences between Eriksen's artwork and my own.

I needed to get that out of the way before reviewing *Tarot of the Elements*. In *Tarot of the Elements*, Lerner and Eriksen aspire to create a tarot based on primordial archetypes. Its symbolism is developed from shamanistic art to express the unconscious forces at work in human consciousness. In the introduction, Lerner analyzes overall numerical and color symbolism. From that I formed the impression that she might steer clear of traditional cartomantic meanings in her meanings of the pip cards. However, I was pleasantly surprised to find that she was respectful of traditional meanings in both her text and the resulting images. In keeping with the decks titles, she names the suit: Fire (in place of Wands); Water (in place of Cups); Air (in place of Swords); and Earth (in place of pentacles or disks.) Artist Ericksen employs icons from the traditional suit names in her illustrations. The writer and artist do balance the focus of the cards on the transformative and subtle energies of the cards, as opposed to pragmatic divinatory meanings, but that works.

Lerner demonstrates knowledge of disciplines, such as astrology, High magick's mathematical formulae and classicism, as well as tarot. That indicates that she has done her homework. Thus, she establishes credentials for herself and her insights. Although she is fond of words like "soul" and "transformation," she develops her rationale from materials known to most serious "mystery" students. However, she can be down to earth. For instance, she writes that Death card can really mean somebody dies, and that it often appears in readings for one who has someone dying in his inner circle. Frankness about that topic (and others) is often missing from more philosophical examinations of tarot. Taken in sum, this makes her come across creditably.

Lerner and Ericksen apply a radical notion to the major arcana that are called Mythical Images. Each of theirs is balanced in all four elements as opposed to one dominant element! The tendency in most tarots is for the later approach. This is by far the most unique quality of *Tarot of the Element*. Their underlying assumption appears to be that since each of these "mythic figures" represents important aspects of human endeavor they should be balanced between all four elements of existence.

Honestly, I've never looked at the major arcana in quite that way before. Let me use the Hanged Man as an example. He is traditionally represented as a figure hanging by his foot with one leg crossed over his knee. I believe that he is most akin to water, as his Golden Dawn moniker "Spirit of Might Waters" indicates. However, I've seen effective representations of that figure with a different elemental association. For instance, Dovilio Brero's Hanged Man in his eponymous deck makes a powerful statement that the slain god is essentially an agricultural artifact by showing a beautiful dead youth bound and strangled amidst sheafs of wheat. Thus Brero's Hanged Man corresponds to an earth rather than water. The hanged man's slaying corresponds to myths of Kings given to feed and thus be reborn through harvests. I can understand that a student might understand earth as being the conduit for regeneration rather then water.[6]

---

[6] Traditionally the Hanged man figure is an inversion of the Emperor. The Emperor's pose is that of the glyph for sulfur (fire.) Water is opposite of fire. As a glyph the upside

Compare these notions to how the Hanged Man in *Tarot of the Four Elements* is depicted. First off, he is called "Shaman." That designation is consistent with other cartomantic interpretations of the card. For instance, Wirth describes him as a Mystic and Initiate whose pure religious feeling is common to all epochs and nations. (Crowley too describes him as an initiate, but that the card itself is essentially a glyph for water.) The Element's Shaman is obviously balanced between Air and Earth. Flame like contours outline his bone structure. His head connects to his penis through his spine is rendered in watery cool blues, indicating the sustaining water of life. His testes are bright red indicating fiery male energy. The figure is obviously animated. One of the frequent attributions of the hanged man is that his body is constricted but his mind is free. The four elements are combined again in the earth in which the figure seems to be plated. There is a pair of watery blue eyes streaming tears of blood (the union of water and fire) in the earth itself yet amidst a field of stars (air elements.)

By integrating all four elements into the major arcana, Lerner and Ericksen do not incorporate elemental dignity into the methodology of *The Tarot of the Four Elements*. For the uninitiated, elemental dignity employs the notion that certain elements harmonize and others do not. Simply put fire and water don't get along; neither does air and earth. So if a card in the suit of Wands comes before one in Cups, the meaning of the Cups card is not in balance. It is a bit more subtle than just flipping the meaning of the card as one does in reversals, since a card that implies a challenge will often become more challenged rather than given a makeover if it is not in elemental harmony. Also, dignity demands the reader look at the overall harmony of energies in the spread. Now, by not having the Major arcana associated with unique elements, the authors

down sulfur sigil also represents perfection of the Great Work, reiterating the meaning of sacrifice "to make sacred."

imply that all elements can be brought into harmony. However, I do imagine from that logic, that a balance of elements would be desirable among the pips in a spread.

The belief that all four elements harmonize, tending to be balanced in a natural state, is optimistic. It implies that things can work out. The primary purpose of divination is to enable the person being read with a strategy for evolution. Starting a reading with the supposition the world is well integrated (and is portrayed in such a state through a number of mythic archetypes) lays groundwork for success in life's journey. All to often tarot readers and other diviners seem to cast their clients' lives in stone. Obviously, this is not what they are supposed to do. The open quality of *Tarot of the Elements* appears designed to encourage individual interpretation and development.

The author is wise enough to know that she and her partner make a departure in their harmonizing of the elements. It's one thing to do something like that because you do not realize that the trumps often have had specific correspondences, it is quite another when you consciously universalize them in hope of liberating people.

The final publication for consideration in this review is the *Toltec Oracle* by Victor Sanchez. Guess what? Someone actually has had the inspiration to create a series of pictographs on card stock, not call it a Tarot, and give us a lucid means of divination. Drop me with a feather or feathered serpent as the case may be! I was a little apprehensive about reviewing this one. I put off looking at it for a long time. I feared that it could be bad on the assumption that this was going to be a tarot based on MezoAmerican culture. Mixing non-European cultural systems with tarot has usually produced pretty disastrous results. Witness all the Orisha tarots. It's a delicate line the creator must walk when drawing correspondences between two systems of meaning. Ideally, the comparisons illuminate each by synthesizing points of resemblance and contrasting differences. Fortunately, Sanchez steers clear of any such pratfall by fashioning an Oracle based on a system of values he well understands. He does not to fit that in the girdle of 22 arcana and 56 pips.

Sanchez is an anthropologist and teacher who has devoted his life to the study of the indigenous peoples of Mexico. His Oracle has 33 cards that reflect Toltec spiritual concepts. There are 20 "Tonalpohualli" cards that correspond to archetypal forces embodied by the twenty days of the Toltec Calendar. The other 13 cards are "Rulers" representing "Poderios" or Toltec elemental deities. Each of the two sets is employed separately before a synthesized interpretation is developed. Sanchez has designed a four-quadrant figure termed the Cross of Ketzelcoatl upon which the cards are thrown in a mandala. A compete reading consists of 4 Tonalpohualli cards with unique meanings derived according to which quadrant they are placed and a ruler card that provides a means of synthesizing the disparate forces.

The technique is solid. It reminds me of Stanislaus de Gautia's technique for interpreting the 22 arcana described in *Tarot of Magicians* that also uses 5 cards in a mandala. However, Sanchez's construction also evokes a technique of throwing Diloggun that divides the divination mat into the four cardinal quadrants. It has a universal appeal. Oracles reverberate with echoes from many cultures, because in matters of sprit mankind more often than not finds him running to and away from the same center.

Sanchez carefully explains the matrix on which his oracle cards are based. In doing so he reveals many similarities between Toltec beliefs and those of other cultures. For instance, I was struck by how much his Toltec belief system corresponded to Yoruba religion. If you changed a few nouns, about 90 percent of the text could have been used to accurately describe Yoruba principles. Its interesting that the Spanish moniker applied to the Toltec deities, Poderios, is virtually the same as what the call Orisha (the deities of Yoruba religion), Poders. The Mesoamerican beliefs described by Sanchez paralleling Yoruba religion include:

> One god who manifests through multiple natural forces.
> Nature as the visible "face of God"
> Personal evolution through actions.
> Liberation through development of consciousness
> Respect of Elders' wisdom
> Worship of the Earth

Sanchez does describe some other beliefs that could be tweaked to fit a Yoruba paradigm. For instance the concept of Ketzelcoatl, a tripartite deity, whose appearance as a feathered serpent embodies the esoteric maxim "as above so below" (a snake crawls on earth, a bird soars the heavens) is close to universal. That concept occurs one way or another in virtually every wisdom path I've encountered. The fact that Sanchez understands it as tri-fold rather than simply dualistic is consistent with finer points of initiatic knowledge in Yoruba spirituality, although in the later case, it is not directly stated. You should just read the Sanchez book for a full explanation of this. As an iguaro, there are some points on which I'm supposed to keep my mouth shut.

My point here is that Sanchez describes a system of understanding that reverberates universally. A vast ocean separates the origin points of the two belief systems I am discussing, yet they are remarkably consistent. I believe that someone whose area of expertise was Asian and not West Afrikan spirituality could probably draw some similar parallels. (In the limited readings I've done on Hindu astrology, many points of similarity also struck me. I have recognized correspondences between geomancy and I Ching with Diloggun divination.)

*The Toltec Oracle* reverberates with many cross-cultural values. At the same time is based on its own coherent worldview. Also, Sanchez has the great good sense to divorce his oracle from fortune telling in its more vulgar sense. An oracle is understood to be a means for divine communication with mankind. Do you really think that Miklantekutli, Yanzan Yeku-Yeku, or even Jesus Christ would want to waste their time explaining that the piece of trade who maxed out your credit cards before going ass and elbows on you really is not coming back? Or do you think that they would perhaps be a shade more in character if they explained why you are alone?

The gap in reality between what value divination should fulfill and what clients expect daunts many a reader. The purpose of a reading is to help a client evolve to a higher level of consciousness. A lot of people just don't see their life journey that way. Tarot can be very useful because it does lend itself to mundane prognostication. (And if we truly adhere to the maxim "as above, so below," Ifa teaches us an asshole is at least as essential if not more so than a mouth.) However, Sanchez has developed a divinatory tool that goes a long way to resisting mundane interrogation. A lot of aspiring diviners would do very, very well to learn this tool. It encourages ethical behavior on the part of a diviner. It does set limits for the client in the types of questions he should ask, and Sanchez clearly explains these in the text. As a reading tool, it is designed to encourage self-reflection and evolution. Sanchez includes specific exercises and behaviors that are consistent with the divinatory meanings of his cards. He also suggests the reader make written record of the readings and suggested behaviors as well as asks questions of himself. The types of things he suggests seem a lot less sappy than a lot of self-improvement rhetoric.

I'm very happy with *The Toltec Oracle*. Sanchez realizes that good sense is also part of divination. Rational and thorough examination of the oracular cards and the individual for whom they are cast encourages deeper understanding. The ultimate goal of such scrutiny is to help reveal that spark of divinity that exists in every person. That brings *Toltec Oracle* in line with the most poignant meaning of Divination.

It is ultimately going to be up to those who read Tarot, rather than those who collect it, to be the ultimate testers of the efficacy of any deck. Obviously you should throw away the cheat sheets at some point. Even Crowley said that the reading of his text *Book of Thoth* could be omitted with profit to the diviner. *Tarot of Fools* is a rollicking account of the history of both tarot and human folly through the lens provided by a classic work of literature. Williams keeps both his viewer's and his own eyes open to what is going on every step of the way. *Tarot of the Imagination* leaves a lot more open to the subjective interpretation of the reader. However, that creates the potential for confusion. A reader needs to be able to create relevant word pictures from the images to link them to the querent's life. Its ambiguousness can cut two ways in enhancing that process. It also presupposes that the reader has a knowledge of European history. (That is probably not a real strong selling point in the U.S.A.) *The Dante Tarot* is a lot more specific in its visual statements. It gains a spiritual richness through the pleasure created by lively harmonies of color and composition. There is enough subtlety in the images that a reader may pick up on idiosyncratic details that lend themselves to specific links of consciousness. However, I cannot truly call it a Tarot. Traditional tarot education may be more of a hindrance than a help with that deck. My overall impression is that *Tarot of the Fours Elements* is that it is a useful deck. It should be fairly easy to read for both the novice and experienced reader. Even though I am uncomfortable with the democratization of elements in the major arcana, the approach to that is consistent and justified by sharp artistic execution. Finally, we leave the tarot genre altogether in *The Toltec Oracle*. By developing it as its own means of divination, Sanchez aspires to introduce the voices of the godhead to many. As a tool of enlightenment, Sanchez's Oracle well exceeds the vast majority of contemporary tarots in being an evolutionary experience and force.

# Reviews

**Queering Creole Spiritual Traditions: Lesbian, Gay, Bisexual and Transgender Participation in African-Inspired Traditions in the Americas,** Randy P. Conner with David Hatfield Sparks
(Harrington Park Press, 2004, 390pp, $29.95)

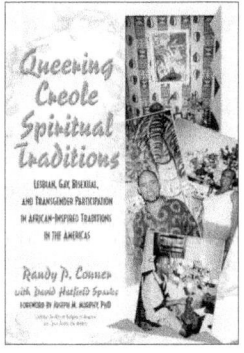

It is refreshing when a book comes along that expands Queer studies into a new area. Randy Conner and David Sparks new book opens the door to one such territory. In *Queering Creole Spiritual Traditions*, Conner and Sparks reveal a world that may not have been exactly secret, but has remained relatively unexamined by religious scholars and Queer theorists. This book examines the lesbian, gay, bisexual and transgender involvement in African-inspired traditions, such as Santeria (Lucumi, Regla de Ocha), Vodou, Candomblé, Macumba, Palo Mayombe, Ifá, Umbanda and Abakúa.

It is difficult to determine the numbers of people practicing Yoruban or Yoruban-inspired religions. Estimates put the number of adherents at approximately 100 million word-wide, placing it within the top 10 most-practiced world religions. By way of comparison, Buddhists are estimated at approximately 360 million and Judaism accounts for 14 million worldwide. Despite this large number of practitioners, very little is known of Yoruban religions outside of those countries and communities where the traditions predominate—e.g. Cuba, Haiti, New Orleans and Florida. Even less known is the involvement of LGBT individuals within the traditions.

While reading *Queering Creole*, the first thought that comes to mind is the sheer scale of LGBT involvement in the religious traditions. One of the book's interviewees, santero (priest) Eric K. Lerner notes that 30-40% percent of practitioners in Cuba and Brazil are homosexual. Considering the estimated number of adherents, such a figure, even if high, makes for a staggering level of LGBT participation. Conner and Sparks show that homosexual inivolvement is more than simply a modern migration toward the tradition. It has been, in fact, a historically significant component of the practice—one likely brought with the slaves from their Yoruban homeland. The authors show that homosexual spiritual houses, including prominent priests, *oungans*, *santeros* and *manbos*, have been common elements historically in both Cuba and Brazil.

Conner and Sparks have spent more than 20 years researching their subject, investigating African-derived spirituality throughout the Americas. The project began when a friend, knowing of their interest in gay spiritual issues, introduced them to two Lucumi practitioners in 1981. Since that encounter, Conner and Sparks have conducted numerous interviews with practitioners in the USA, Cuba, Haiti and Brazil.

The book begins with a detailed discussion of sexual and gender complexity in Africa. They highlight the marked differences between the conception of sexuality and gender in Yoruban cultural and the Western. The authors also raise the inherent problems of cultural anthropology and the dangers of imposing one's own conceptions onto other cultures.

This accusation has been leveled against the study of gender complexity in particular. Conner and Sparks raise the issue and then make a surprising and compelling counter-argument. They suggest that the negative critiquing of gender analysis in cultural anthropology may itself derive from homophobia and culturally inculcated resistance within the critics.

The book proceeds with a discussion of several of the key divinities within the various traditions. They show how the divine itself at times exhibits gender complexity. Through myths and stories surrounding the divinities, they show the evolution of practitioners' understanding of the gods and goddesses.

Conner and Sparks provide a detailed analysis of various aspects of the traditions and how they intersect with LGBT issues. In addition to the historical participation of homosexuals, they examine AIDS and HIV/AIDS education programs in Brazil, and the participation of transgendered individuals. Despite the comparatively large numbers of LGBT participants, there also exists a strongly rooted resistance among some practitioners. Conner and Sparks discuss spiritual houses that prohibit LGBT involvement and the arguments behind such prohibitions. They also examine certain historical taboos against gender complex persons and women from taking up certain tradition roles within the spiritual practice, such as playing the *bata*, or sacred drums, an integral component in many ceremonies.

The majority of the book is given over to discussions of the numerous interviews the authors conducted over more than twenty years. These they break into two sections, the first of practitioners and priests and the second of artists, musicians and performers who have a connection to African-diasporic traditions. The interview subjects dramatically demonstrate the involvement of LGBT peoples in the spiritual traditions—both contemporary and historically through acknowledgement of their lineage.

Having previously written *Cassell's Encyclopedia of Queer Myth, Symbol and Spirit*, the authors are ideally suited to their subject. They approach the project with academic rigor, while producing an incredibly readable book. The publication of *Queering Creole Spiritual Traditions* is a landmark in LGBT studies and a watershed in the anthropological examination of gender complexity in spiritual practice.

**The Shamanic Way of the Bee: Ancient Wisdom and Healing Practices of the Bee Masters,** Simon Buxton
(Inner Traditions, 2004, 206pp, $20.00)

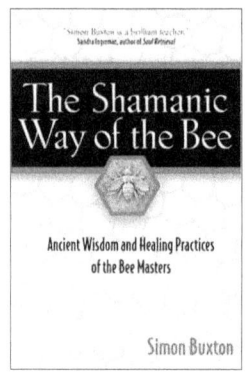

The Bee Master Knows: BUZZ WORD: READ THIS BOOK!!!

Simon Buxton has turned out one of the best books that this reviewer has had the pleasure of reading in a long time. When I was assigned this book, I will confess that I had some doubts and even postponed reading it as long as I could. I had thought, "Oh boy, more new age pablum." I am so delighted to confess that I was very, very wrong. The content is brilliantly presented by an entertaining storyteller of no small ability. The Shamanic Way of the Bee is simply one of those books that, if you should pick up, will have a very hard time putting down.

There is a nice rhythmic flow to the dialogue and one hardly realizes that thirty pages have flown by:

> After my bath, I headed out to the orchard. With the Gate of Transition before me once more, and the trepidation of crossing its

threshold now long extinct, I passed through, feeling that the mystic green landscape beyond had a far richer connection to my soul. Kipling reverberated through my mind: 'Our England is a garden.' Here were still, rural regions, peaceful and beloved, where tranquil rivers flowed, rolling meadows shone in the sun, and castles and cathedrals sat serenely, much as they do in the Britain of storybooks. A little farther a field were grim moors, abrupt hills, and threatening islands. And beyond and behind this outer landscape—I now knew this with certainty—there was a hidden world all around me, a world full of magic, mystery, and adventure, and I considered how the character of the British people was molded and informed as much by the quiet secluded valleys and the steep crags as the mysteries that emanate from behind the trembling veil that separates the unseen world from this one.

Mr. Buxton tells the story of how he got involved in, not only the keeping of bees, but also the mysteries of the lore that surrounds the tradition of bee keeping. It is an odyssey of his personal journey into the realms of the shaman, how he was selected, and is a worthy recapitulation of his apprenticeship with a mysterious 'Don Juan Matus' type character named 'Bridge'. Even though one will find similarities between this account and the work of Carlos Castaneda, there are some striking differences as well—the context of Celtic, Welsh and British lore not being among the least. There are also adventures with intriguing characters such as the Bee Mistress and her Melissae. There are the ordeals and the trysts and the exhilarating intoxication of those who are totally absorbed in their actions.

The author begins his account by telling us about his seemingly unfortunate experience with encephalitis at the tender age of nine. The doctors had given up on him and told his parents that they should resign themselves to the inevitable. However, the fates that oversee this life have a different design for young Simon. A kindly man of great experience, who had befriended the young boy two years before, known as 'Herr Professor' facilitates a miraculous recovery by employing healing techniques shunned by modern science but long known amongst those mysterious figures sometimes called shamans. From this time onward he teaches the young boy the intimacies of the Austrian forests and the connection that we each have with the great ebb and flow of life. Herr Professor is also a keeper of bees and this provides the foreshadowing of the author's future experiences.

Mr. Buxton describes how in 1986 he wondered onto the bee keeping estate of 'Bridge', and after an interesting ordeal, that I'll not spoil by revealing, Simon becomes the apprentice of Bridge and begins to learn the ways of bee keeping and the magical and matriarchal life of the hive.

This book is chock full of interesting anecdotes that reveal not only the wisdom of the 'path of pollen', but one abundant with the love of life and a ready comprehension of its mysteries. Although, I ordinarily would ordinarily give a fuller recounting of the story in terms of the development of plot, setting, characters and so on ...this read is simply too fast, and it would be unfair for those of you who are wise enough to take my advice and READ THIS BOOK, to spoil the majesty revealed in this true and moving tale.

Simon Buxton is still, to this day, a beekeeper and also a teacher in various techniques of shamanism. Anyone interested in learning from keen mind should contact Sacred Trust.

Further information can be found at www.sacredtrust.org

I give this one a five out of five stars and will conclude by saying that if you don't go get this book and read it, you are missing out. You can read ten technical treatises on shamanism and magick and not get half of the information content that you will find in this charming and compelling tale.

## Jesus and the Shamanic Tradition of Same-Sex Love, Will Roscoe
(Suspect Thoughts, 2004, 224pp, $16.95)

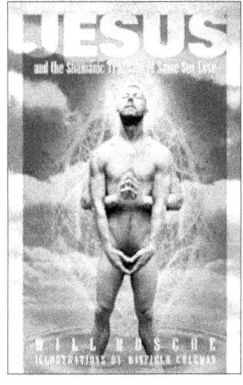

While a graduate student at Columbia University, Mortan Smith was invited to catalogue the holdings of the Mar Saba monastery library, near Jerusalem. Smith began his work in the Spring of 1958. He discovered several interesting, though not earth shattering, manuscripts among the collection, including new scholia of Sophocles. This was the case until, in his words, an "afternoon near the end of my stay, I found myself in my cell, staring incredulously at a text written in a tiny scrawl." (Smith, The Secret Gospel of Mark, 1973, p. 12) This text, written in the blank back pages of a 17th century edition of Voss's *Epistolae genuinae S. Ignatii Martyris*, purported to be a partial transcription of a much older manuscript—a letter from Clement of the Stromateis to a follower identified only as Theodore.

Known more commonly as Clement of Alexandria, the author was an important second century neo-platonic church theologian. In the Mar Saba letter, Clement is responding to questions raised by his follower stemming from a debate the latter had with the Carpocratians, a heterodoxical sect. The questions posed by Theodore relate to a variant version of the gospel of Mark used by the Carpocratians in their arguments. Clement does not attack the authenticity of this 'secret gospel of Mark.' Instead he tells Theodore that it is held by the Alexandrian Church, who utilizes it in their initiations, and then proceeds to quote from his personal copy.

The 1972 publication of Smith's findings in two editions, one general and one scholarly, caused a stir in biblical academic circles. Though debate continues, many scholars now accept the letter as authentic. Yuri Kuchinsky has set out a detailed case demonstrating the near impossibility of the document being a modern forgery—an accusation leveled by some. Indeed, the letter is included in the scholarly edition of Clement's collected works.

What remains more controversial is Smith's exegesis of the text and subsequent interpretation. Smith proposed that the text of Secret Mark alluded to a secret baptismal rite conducted by Jesus. Within the ritual, the postulant was dressed only in a single piece of linen (similar to a shroud) over his naked body. In the context of the baptizing Jesus was able to transfer (directly) to his disciple a direct vision of the kingdom of God.

The manuscript's discovery and resulting scholarly debate is fascinating. Roscoe does a superb job retelling the story and capturing in detail the import of discovery and the debate surrounding it. He also provides a clear analysis of Smith's interpretations of Secret Mark— bringing into the discussion many supporting instances (and telling omissions) from the canonical synoptic gospels. *Jesus & the Shamanic Tradition* is, in part, a scholarly work and adheres to the necessary rigors of that discipline. Though some readers may indeed find the level of detail daunting, it provides a necessary background from which Roscoe jumps into the interpretative second half of the book.

At the outset of his work Roscoe is careful to point that his is not (another) book retelling the life and a gay Jesus. "For the record," Roscoe writes, "I do not believe that [The Secret Gospel of Mark] provides any evidence regarding Jesus' emotional or sexual orientation." He does, however, propose that it "provides compelling evidence that the first Christians, including Jesus, engaged in mystical practices involving intimate same-sex contact." For Roscoe the moments of the mystical (shamanic) Jesus glimpsed in the Secret Gospel of Mark provide for gay people "an opportunity to read themselves into the heritage of Western religion and spirituality as a whole."

Jumping off of Smith's interpretation, Roscoe theorizes that Jesus practiced a baptismal ritual based on same-sex contact, yes perhaps sexual in nature, in which he imparted a mystical vision of heaven or the kingdom of God. This is not dissimilar from other shamanic practices in other parts of the world. Roscoe spends a good portion of the book discussing these other traditions and distilling from them similarities which help in an understanding of the conduct of the mystical initiating Jesus.

Roscoe is a respected scholar. His earlier works have included studies of gender and third-genders among the Zuni, Africans and Native Americans. He brings his unique wealth of knowledge to bear on his interpretive arguments relating to Jesus as a shaman, without allowing it to overwhelm his core discussion.

Secret Mark seems tied to gay spirituality. Smith's book came into Roscoe's hands from those of Harry Hay, the legendary founding father of the modern gay rights movement and the radical faeries. "I think there's something in here we should be concerned with," he told Roscoe cryptically.

His is a unique and at times powerfully beautiful interpretation of *agape* (Love). The egalitarian notion of love expounded by Hay during his life, and its connection to the mystical side of Jesus' teachings and ritual practices, was brought into sharp relief for Roscoe when the AIDS epidemic hit the gay community. "It was the epidemic that enabled me to see the real significance of the Secret Gospel of Mark. Love between equals and sames—agape, subject-subject love—is heaven and earth."

Roscoe has set himself no small task... yet he carries it out flawlessly. He grounds his revolutionary theory in canonical and apocryphal scriptural sources and teams this with an expert's background in cross-cultural anthropology of gender and sexuality.

*For more information see:*
Wieland Willker's Secret Gospel of Mark Homepage
http://www.user.uni-bremen.de/~wie/Secret/secmark_home.html

Yuri Kuchinsky's SECRET MARK webpage
http://www.trends.ca/~yuku/bbl/secmk.htm

**Psychic Vampire Codex: A Manual of Magick and Energy Work,**
Michelle Belanger
(Red Wheel/Weiser, 2004, 284pp, $19.95)

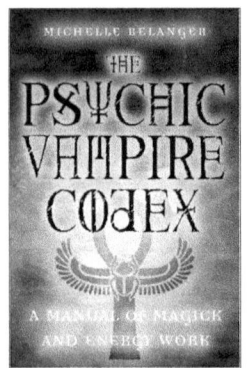

Let me begin this review with a caveat: This was a difficult review for me to write since I have little interest in the life of vampires, and even as pop-culture curiosities, my interest in them has been marginal at best. In fact, my exposure has remained rather confined to Dracula, and "The Fearless Vampire Killers"

(Strains of: *It's Too Late to Love Sharon Tate.*)

I'm not a person who is very drawn to gothic culture but can confess somewhat of an incidental interest in 'Goth' as the product of over three generations of the mass consumption of television and comic books. Shows like Buffy The Vampire Slayer,

Angel and Charmed feed the current newbies with all sorts of regurgitated fanciful images …with, I might confess, superior special effects. In my own generation, this was represented by Barnabas Collins of Dark Shadows fame, or Grandpa and Eddie Munster. One can easily see a difference in attitude toward what has come to be known as gothica. ..After all, Batman USED TO BE a funny guy.

Some have said that Anne Rice put it over the top with her Interview With A Vampire. Such strong imagery has found a resonation with a growing number of people as the 'Children of the Night' are finally coming out of the broom closet. Enter Michelle Belanger's: "The Psychic Vampire's Codex". (Weiser Books 2004) This was initially a work that emerged from cyberspace, as computers created a means for people of like interest to communicate and organize. The Codex has been circulating on the web for a few years as a general ethical guide but the recently published work has a ton of background material and additional information that makes this a 'must have' for those with an interest in vampires as a 'real' feature on the culture-scape. As I indicated above, it has a certain anthropological value in that it portrays a modular representation of a mind-set in today's world.

This book is for the person coming into the vampire lifestyle. It is apologetic to some degree and establishes some guidelines. It gives one an insight into the vampire community: the way it has organized itself, what it feels it has to offer for those who participate in it, the 'laws of the land' as it were and so on.

As the founder of House Kheperu and the articulator of the Kheprian Mysteries, Belanger has been a significant focalizer in the Vampire (Vampyre or Kheprian) culture and so is able to define a unique and authoritative perspective in this work. Owing to this, she quite definitely presents an 'insider's view.' I found her writing style to be fluid and accessible, which made this review far less a chore than it could have been otherwise. For that she has my gratitude.

She also illustrates a broad base of learning and uses the book to put forth numerous ideas for those with interests beyond vampires. There is a great deal of information on psychic energy and the role of the 'vampire' not merely as a parasitic figure, but as the answer to the detriments of 'surplus energy':

> "The basic premise of the Codex is that all being participate in a universal cycle, and a psychic vampire's relation to energy is an integral part of this participation.
>
> ...Taking energy away can be as helpful and healing as giving energy to another person. Too often energy becomes blocked and stagnant, and this blocked energy must be removed from a person's system to maintain a healthy flow. Furthermore, when energy is removed from a person, their system naturally responds by generating more energy to replace it. This new energy is fresher and more vital than that which was removed, and typically the individual feels cleansed, refreshed, and renewed." p. 40-41

What follows are numerous psychic energy exercises and techniques culled from a wide variety of sources for grounding, centering, meditation, and visualization and so in this sense offers some practical endeavor for numerous disciplines that extends beyond the vampire community in particular to those more general practitioners of the occult. As I said at the beginning, for those with an interest in these subject matters, this is a very nice addition for one's personal curriculum. I give it a 4 out of 6 fangs.

### Novice to Master: An Ongoing Lesson in the Extent of My Own Stupidity, Soko Morinaga
(Wisdom, 2004, 154pp, 11.95)

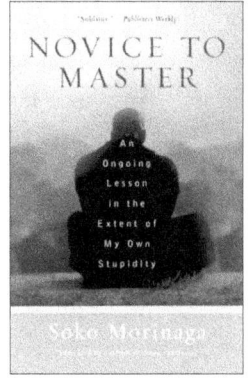

Occasionally one is lucky enough to come upon a book which can be described by a single word: Wonderful! Subtitled "an ongoing lesson in the extent of my own stupidity," *Novice to Master* takes one through the subtle, water-flowing philosophy of Zen, while avoiding being too philosophical or too religious or too Zen. Soko Morinaga (1925-1995) received the seal Dharma transmission from Sesso Ota Roshi. Morinaga served as the head of Hanazono University, the primary training school of the Rinzai sect. Morinaga's book is first-and-foremost an autobiography following the author's journey from his adolescence to entering his first monastery to becoming a Zen master. Through his tale Morinaga imparts wisdom that is easy to access and based on traditional Zen commonsense. The reader also receives unique glimpses into the heart of Zen Buddhist monastic life—in a way that envelopes the reader in the tradition as opposed to allowing otherness to block one's access. Morinaga is a gifted storyteller, self-deprecating, where appropriate, and possessing a perfect sense of timing. There are gems and Dharma treasures throughout the book: "You must puzzle out your own unripeness," Moringaga points out. This book is for anyone interested in engaging a practical and, simultaneously, spiritual life. The beginner and the advance student will both come away from it with much in hand. This is a story of a life and, more importantly, the wisdom gained from a full and spiritual life. This is not a book of esoteric teachings or intricate extrapolations of sutra. This is a work for all interested in an engaged life. Morinaga's tale is a masterpiece of 20th spiritual writing.

**Immortal Light,** Swami Amar Jyoti
(Truth Consciousness, 2004, 492pp, $24.95)

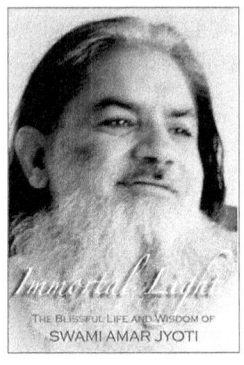

Swami Amar Jyoti was one of the Indian gurus who brought Yoga and Vedanta to the West in the latter part of the 20th century. Jyoti split his time between Indian and the United States. He established ashrams in both Pune, India and Boulder, Colorado, USA. Jyoti's personal philosophy was of a Divine godhead that was both Mother and Father. Like other spiritual leaders of his era, Jyoti attempted to meld the central spiritual cores of various historic religious teachers together into a single universal philosophy. *Immortal Light* is a spiritual autobiography pulled together from various talks Jyoti gave on his life and spiritual awakening. The work is well edited by long-time Jyoti disciple Sita Stuhlmiller. Despite being drawn from Satsangs (spiritual discourses) given over the course of several years, *Immortal Light* avoids the disjointed feel that often flaws such compilations. The work follows chronologically Jyoti's spiritual quest, journey to the Himalayas and eventual spiritual awakening. His tales impart wisdom gained from his interaction with his own teachers and spiritual guides he met along the way toward his own enlightenment experience. Jyoti through his discourses on his own life also introduces his spiritual philosophy drawing on both traditional Yoga and Vedanta while bringing in his own syncretic philosophy of a universal spirituality.

# Down by Dull Canal

*Cabell McLean*

*Originally appeared in* Heroin Addict #5, 1983, M. Houston, editor; and read at *St. Mark's Fire Benefit 1983.*

Young tough from the past runs out and with slow finger's ambiguous movement asks if I want to? Then down and in off the street in a smell of stagnant water up the old brick alley a puff of dying breath under the door his last easy gesture coming in a flash of milk white light. Rank musty parchment smell of wollen flowers might have been mixed up in my mind under the brown fog of a winter's dawn we thought you might have been lost the words seemed to stand out loud as a swelling organ note fulsome and resonant in the violet air

> A blush of blue on grey slate cliffs,
> it sings to you no hiding place.

When at last I reached the top of the rope a climax of excitement would pass through me to be up amongst the rafters for there you feel free after so much pulling and straining with my arms heavy with the fragrance of grey flannel trousers the blue veins standing out softly a hint of violet in the air just beyond damask paper curtains. Snow plums on the manicured lawn red leather furniture and tarnished sliver laced parchment lampshades and your shadow at evening rising to meet you. The food counter in a fur coat in late winter I remember each separate hair glistening and alive as if the animal had just been skinned. The translucent jam made from white cherries and a tray of tea in the warmth of the fireplace as I lay there watching the mauve glow on the ceiling and hating the still stifling silence. "I was neither living nor dead and I knew nothing." Outside I saw crests of rooves sticking up through the snow like the bones of a rotting fish covered with salt. Speckled brown quail egg warmed on the oven lawn chairs were left out in the gardens and down by the dull canal the snow covered grandstands looked like an empty box of chocolates still trimmed with frilly papers. Whispering little youth ran out from the past lurking in old cottage by the river now covered in mint and ivy.

A naked aggressive last breath glided noiselessly
as soft rhythmic waves of grey flannel sickness passed over me.

Glass in the darkening grass hurry up please it's time the feel of steel stairs beneath me and a vague touching my side hoping to feel ribs as silky water music came to me as a spidery tinkle filtered through a thousand cobwebs or the sound of some mermaid blowing on her comb in her cave beneath the sea. A white arm the muscles tight and knotted and tiny hands pushing on my numb and shattered shoulder hoping to feel bone.

I began to float away through a great cloud of agony.
In the stillness of late morning he softly wept over me.

Tiniest tingling feeling of water touching my ribs disappeared in
the cool thin air and emerald stink of the floating docks and cinnamon
winds of Mexico across the water salmon pink velvet grey flannel
trousers the imitation classical ruins looked like a golf course over distant
mountains *un beaucoup passionment* now beautifully missing the clouds of
time going backwards it seemed once again a happy place. But I was
grieved over vague uneasy feeling of universal damage and loss faded
water color feeling the fragrance of someone's hair laced with cinnamon
and patchouli a desert winds racing coldly up the legs of my new grey
flannel trousers sprays of early apple across damask paper curtain the sun
shone through and made stars tingle in my eyes. Though dirty armchair
damage had faded and the windows were closed a climax of excitement
over took me and water music came up to me among the rafters the reek
of opium unmistakable in the cold floating corruptly on the room's
velvet curtains a door opening with a gust of time wind tingling sweet
ache in my legs as I dangle from the ceiling beams in the raw wet
summer to stand upon the brown steel bridge watching two trains
running down the line of track, bright little points glittering in the purple
night spiced dust in red hairs by the dark water a thrill of pleasure and of
pain kicking legs to fight free twisting painfully locked in bubble escaping
from shapeless mouths everywhere contracting in golden green spasms in
the yellow mud the colors squirm through his body arched like water
weed stretching up to grasp my excited legs glittering semen fingers
around my ankle dragging me down with a horrible writhing anxious sort
of love as I tried to cry out, "Fear death by water! Fear death!" The icy
water on my sweating frantic body making the curious thrill of terror the
shining hazel jelly in lumps by the water fear death by pleausure fear
death.

He found a bare tree, and he climbed up
into the branches, tied the rope, and then jumped.

They found him the next day, and the whole tree was hung with Judas flowers in red and yellow. Judas had red hair, you know. Here's a picture of Judas hanging like a fish from the judas tree with the red hair and red flowers all around. This is how a hanged man looks: his head lolls to one side, shudder of pain and regret, the legs kick spasmodically, and a silver light pops in his eyes.

www.ingramcontent.com/pod-product-compliance
Lightning Source LLC
Chambersburg PA
CBHW071713170526
45165CB00005B/2000